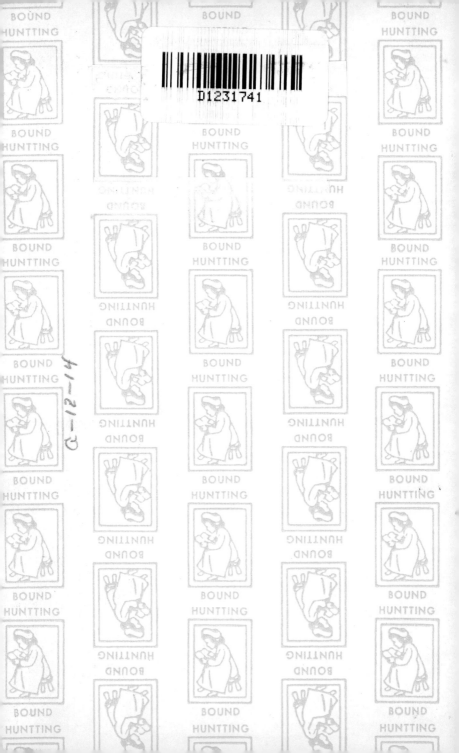

OAK and IVY

A Biography of Paul Laurence Dunbar

OAK and IVY

A BIOGRAPHY OF

PAUL LAURENCE DUNBAR

BY

ADDISON GAYLE, Jr.

A PERSPECTIVE BOOK

Dorothy Sterling, Editorial Consultant

DOUBLEDAY & COMPANY, INC.

GARDEN CITY, NEW YORK

He sang of love when earth was young,
And Love, itself, was in his lays.
But ah, the world, it turned to praise
A jingle in a broken tongue.

CONTENTS

INTRODUCTION

The year was eighteen ninety-two. Snow covered the narrow unpaved streets of Dayton, Ohio, hiding the shingled houses under a blanket of gleaming whiteness. A messenger, a scarf pulled tightly around his neck, a package tucked securely under his arm, walked up to the stoop of the house belonging to Matilda Dunbar and her son, Paul. Matilda watched the messenger arrive. She reached the door at the first ring, opened it wide, ushered the young man inside. Before he could say, "Package for Mr. Paul Laurence Dunbar," she had taken it from his gloved hand.

The package was from the United Brethren Publishing House in Dayton and contained copies of Dunbar's first book of poems, *Oak and Ivy*. The messenger was unaware of this. However, he did know that the package contained something of importance. All the way over, while plodding through the snow, he had wondered what the package held and who the man was to whom it belonged. Watching the old woman fondling it so carefully, he asked hurriedly, as though afraid that the words might not come at a slower pace: "What is this Dunbar? Is he a doctor, a lawyer, a preacher?"

Matilda smiled. "Paul," she replied, her eyes lighting up, "why Paul is just an elevator boy." She paused, the lights seemed to glow brighter in her eyes. Finally, she continued with a burst of pride, "And . . . and a poet!"

An elevator boy and a poet! For the rest of his life and long after his death, Dunbar would be known by these two terms. Biographers would write warmly about the early days when he operated the elevator in the Callahan Building, where he composed some of his best poems while being frequently interrupted to pick up passengers on a distant floor.

He was a poet long before he became an elevator boy—some would say that he had been born a poet. This was not quite true, although he began rhyming words at the age of six. Some of his biographers would say much later that he was a great poet; but this also was not true. He might have been a great poet if he had been allowed to write the kind of poetry he wished to write. A few years before his death, while visiting a fellow poet, James Weldon Johnson, he seemed to recognize this fact himself. "I have kept doing the same things over and over," he told Johnson. "I have never done the things that I wanted to do."

There was sadness in this statement, and he expressed it often in his lifetime. He believed that he was held down, kept from fulfilling his promise by an unseen fate like that which controlled the lives of his characters in his novel, *The Sport of the Gods*. However, the fate that controlled him was not invisible. It was composed of many forces and many people, and it had operated to make him an elevator boy against his wishes. Before accepting the position at the Callahan Building he had tried to gain work more fitting for a high school graduate.

He tried factories, warehouses, and even newspapers, many of which had published his poems while he was still a student at Central High School. He asked for positions such as clerk, accountant, or receptionist.

At each place, the employer or a representative gave him the same answer, implied if not always spoken, "We have no jobs of this kind for Negroes." Dayton, in the 1900s, was a small town. People knew one another, and hardly anything of importance occurred that did not reach the ears of the townsfolk.

Almost everyone knew of Paul Laurence Dunbar. They knew he had been the only black student enrolled at Central High School; that he had been elected president of the senior class; that he had served as editor of the school paper, and that he was considered to be one of the town's most promising young men. Still, they turned him down with the words, "We don't hire Negroes for this kind of work."

During slavery, Dayton had held no men in bondage. With the exception of the Dunbar family, there were few black people in the town. Most of the townsmen knew of black people only through knowing the Dunbars, who were respected as good citizens. Yet these men believed the myths that other men had spread about black people. Myths that said that blacks were simple, childish creatures who had to have special homes, special eating places, special seats on public transportation, and special jobs.

What did it matter if Dunbar had been a good student? Was he not still a black man? Of what importance was it that he wrote poetry? Did not poetry contain rhythm, and did not all black people have an abundance of rhythm? Moreover, did he not write dialect poetry, and was not dialect the language of a simple, childish people?

Dunbar did indeed write dialect poetry; and in it he catered to the worst of the Southern myths. He wrote of simple slaves who loved their masters, of childish people whose only desire was to go coon hunting, to take the banjo down from the wall, to serve their white masters and mistresses with loyalty and devotion, and to party from "sun down to sun up."

He knew, however, that very little of what he wrote in dialect was true. How could he believe in the simplicity

of black people when there had been such men of the race
as Frederick Douglass, Henry Highland Garnet, and Nat
Turner? Such women as Sojourner Truth, Harriet Tubman,
and Mary Church Terrell? Had he been free to write often
of such people in pure English, his poetry would have been
far different from what it was. "I never wanted to write
dialect," he confessed to James Weldon Johnson; and in
poem after poem he despaired over the fact that others
dictated the route that his youthful imagination was to take.
A clue to his feelings on this point may be found in the poem,
Misapprehension:

> *Out of my heart, one day, I wrote a song,*
> *   With my heart's blood imbued,*
> *Instinct with passion, tremulously strong,*
> *   With grief subdued;*
> *   Breathing a fortitude*
> *   Pain-bought.*
> *And one who claimed much love for what I wrought,*
> *   Read and considered it,*
> *   And spoke:*
> *"Ay, brother,—'t is well writ,*
> *   But where's the joke?"*

The joke was missing in a great deal of Dunbar's poetry.
Though he wrote of love, nature, and death, the white
world ignored these, praising him and making him famous
for what he called "jingles in a broken tongue." Few noticed the "note of sadness" that crept into much of the poetry he wrote in standard English. Like Thomas Gray, the
English poet, much of his poetry is about death, the thought
of dying, and the wish to die. In a letter written to a friend
in 1894, he expressed such a wish openly: "There is only

one thing left to be done, and I am too big a coward to do that."

He continued to live and to write poetry, short stories, and novels. And he lived in a world in which men, not free themselves, continued to restrict his freedom. They not only forced him to write about black people, but in addition, they forced him to write about black people as they wanted black people to be. He acquiesced because, as he said, "I had to get a hearing."

The hearing cost him dearly. To be sure, it brought fame and fortune; but it also brought despondency, heartbreak, and pain. His sickness, his alcoholic problems, the breakup of his marriage—all resulted from the terrible price he had to pay to get a hearing. In a country where black poets and writers suffer under the impulses and control of other men, none suffered so much as Dunbar. The extent of his pain may be measured in the lines from *Conscience and Remorse*:

> "Good-bye," I said to my conscience—
> "Good-bye for aye and aye,"
> And I put her hands off harshly,
> And turned my face away;
> And conscience smitten sorely
> Returned not from that day.

But his conscience did not stray far. It came back again and again to haunt him and to force him to fight against those who had restricted his freedom. During those times he wrote poems like *The Haunted Oak,* which describes the lynching of a black man; short stories like *The Lynching of Jube Benson,* which assails the act of lynching; and novels like *The Sport of the Gods,* which reveals the true nature of the plantation system. In poems and stories like these, he gave the lie to all he had written of the wonderful life "wey down souf" during slavery.

However, such times were too few. The poems and stories of that kind were inadequate compensation for his suffering. When he died at the age of thirty-four, he had outlived his creative talent by ten years. To millions who read his works, the terms by which his mother announced his calling—elevator boy and poet—were adequate to his career. Others were not so easily satisfied. They knew that he might have been described as a great poet and that this recognition had been denied him because of his color. The nation had painted a picture of him to which it demanded that he conform. That picture was to stand for all of his people, and it was one of a simple-minded child, a buffoon.

He was not a buffoon, nor was he an entertainer; and he spent the best years of his life attempting to convince people of this fact. The failure of this attempt and the tension between being a poet and an entertainer formed the major conflict of his life. "Most men," wrote Henry David Thoreau, "live lives of quiet desperation." And although Dunbar's life was seldom quiet, it was extremely desperate. It was a life filled with disappointment and dashed hopes; a life in which the great battles were lost—those with his publishers and critics, and those with love and death.

Despite his shortcomings, or perhaps because of them, he won acclaim in the eyes of millions of black men. They too led lives of quiet desperation. They too had been forced to sell their souls in order to survive in a country which constantly deemed them unworthy. They too had suffered a loss of freedom. Of all his poems, perhaps the one they admired the most was that in which he put into words not only the terror of his own life, but of theirs as well:

We wear the mask that grins and lies,
It hides our cheeks and shades our eyes,—
This debt we pay to human guile;
With torn and bleeding hearts we smile,
And mouth with myriad subtleties.

Why should the world be over wise,
In counting all our tears and sighs?
Nay, let them only see us, while
    We wear the mask.

We smile, but, O great Christ, our cries
To thee from tortured souls arise.
We sing, but oh the clay is vile
Beneath our feet, and long the mile;
But let the world dream otherwise,
    We wear the mask!

I

OH, MOTHER RACE

Be proud, my Race, in mind and soul:
Thy name is writ on Glory's scroll
In characters of fire.

The great battle was set for the latter part of April 1892. Neither of the opponents had met the other; neither had been told that the other would be present. Paul Laurence Dunbar was not to know, until a few moments before the battle commenced, that his opponent was the scholarly, argumentative, gentleman from Toledo, Ohio, Dr. W. C. Chapman. Dr. Chapman was not to know until the last moment—in fact, not until he had taken his turn at the rostrum—that he was to confront Paul Laurence Dunbar, "the boy poet" from Dayton, Ohio, in person.

The newly formed West End Club, a literary society in Toledo, had been chosen as the battleground. Dr. Chapman, a member and one of the founding fathers, had recently completed a trip throughout the South. On this trip, he prepared a paper, "The Negro in the South," in which he recorded his observations of Southern Negro life. This paper he was to read before the assembly that night.

Dunbar, on the other hand, had been asked to give a reading. Requests for readings came frequently now, calling him from his elevator at the Callahan Building, and he tried to fulfill each engagement. The readings supplemented his salary of four dollars a week and, in addition, offered him the opportunity to sell copies of his first volume of poems,

Oak and Ivy, which had been off the press for only four months.

By this time he was an old hand at readings. He knew which numbers went over well with his audience. *The Rivals, The Cornstalk Fiddle, A Banjo Song,* and *October* were among the crowd pleasers. He had chosen all of these, plus others, for the reading at the West End Club.

Fresh from a reading in Detroit, where he had appeared at some Negro churches, he was met at the Toledo depot by Charles Thatcher, one of Dayton's most respected young attorneys. He had first met Thatcher on one of those days when it seemed that fate was inclined to favor him with her blessings. While sitting at his elevator, hastily scribbling lines on a pad, one ear attuned to the elevator bell, he was approached by Mrs. Frank Conover whose husband, a lawyer, had an office in the building. She noticed him scribbling rapidly in his notebook. Upon seeing her, he thrust the notebook carefully aside and leaped to his feet, an embarrassed grin on his face. Curious as to what a Negro elevator boy might be writing while at work, she questioned him. At first he refused to answer, mumbling inaudibly so that she could not make out his words. When she persisted, and he was convinced that she would not go away until she had discovered his secret, he sheepishly produced his poems.

Each surprised the other. Mrs. Conover had read his poems in the Dayton *Herald;* had even clipped some of them. She was very happy to meet the young poet. From that point on, she kept up with his career, and when *Oak and Ivy* was published, her name was among the first on the subscription list that Dunbar attached to the wall of the elevator. Upon reading it, Mrs. Conover was so pleased with the slender volume of poetry that she sent a copy to Charles Thatcher as a Christmas gift.

After reading the poems, Thatcher wrote Dunbar, asking for information about his life, his work, and his aspirations. Dunbar replied from his post at the elevator. He not only wrote a brief autobiographical sketch, but also informed the lawyer that he gave readings in and around Dayton, and that he would soon be going to Detroit for that purpose. He hoped, he added, "to get other engagements in the near vicinity."

"Please stop off in Toledo on your way to Detroit," Thatcher replied immediately; and about the middle of May 1892, Dunbar made the first of his many trips to that city. Toledo, in the late nineteenth century, was a major industrial city. One section was filled with shops, office buildings, and manufacturing concerns; the other consisted of tree-lined streets and fashionable homes. Here, the wealthy and the near-wealthy families lived. Toledo was to play a major role in Dunbar's career. Many of the men who were to aid him in his climb to fame were residents of the city and all were important men.

By April 1893 Paul Laurence Dunbar had published a book and his poems and short stories had appeared in the Dayton papers and in a few Midwestern magazines. And these accomplishments brought him local recognition—making his name familiar to those who lived in and around Dayton.

Dr. Chapman was one of those who had heard of him; and in his paper to be read before the West End Club, Chapman was to refer to him repeatedly. Of all this, Dunbar knew nothing. That night, riding along in the horse-drawn buggy with the lawyer at his side, he went over in his mind, during a lull in the conversation, a few phrases of the poems he would recite. As the carriage neared the entrance of the club, Thatcher, a twinkle of amusement in his eyes, interrupted the poet's train of thought, informing him that a Dr. W. C. Chapman of Toledo was one of the night's speakers.

As they stepped onto the sidewalk, Thatcher continued: "My committee is counting on you to provide the lighter side of the program; I don't imagine the doctor's paper will be especially interesting." And as they made their way into the spacious hall, the lawyer whispered, "We're the only ones who know you're going to appear."

They took seats near the far door. On the platform, the president of the club presented Dr. Chapman to the packed audience. Somewhat self-consciously, he strode to the rostrum amid light applause. He glanced at the crowd about him, bowed from the waist, straightened out his papers on the mahogany stand, and before commencing to speak, for a few seconds stared majestically into the eyes of his audience. Dunbar watched his movements. Like the others, he was impatient for the man to begin. He hoped that Chapman would tell of the black man's struggle under great adversity, of the poverty and persecution under which he labored daily, and of how necessary it was that men of good will try to alleviate these conditions.

Dr. Chapman said nothing of the kind. Instead of being favorably disposed towards the Negro, he was his cynical foe. The Negro in the South, he noted, was "lazy, shiftless, cunning, and childlike." He was ignorant, happily so, and incapable of being taught. His condition was bad, but he had brought this condition upon himself. The light of civilization, the doctor went on, of learning, of culture had not penetrated the dark corridors of the Negro's mind, and there was little chance that it would ever do so.

He had warmed to his subject. With a true feel for the speaker's art, he paused allowing his words to sink in, looked his audience once again in the eye, and, ignorant of the fact that Dunbar sat in the audience, injected the name of the poet into his address. Paul Dunbar, the Dayton poet, he argued was no exception to the general rule. Instead he was "a freak of nature: his poems are no proof that Negroes are teachable."

Dunbar fidgeted on his seat. The anger was visible in his clear dark eyes. It was difficult for him to believe that such words were coming from a rostrum around which so many distinguished people had gathered. Moreover, they were coming from a man who was not only learned, but a respected citizen of the city. He blinked his eyes. He thought about Chapman's words, not so much those that pertained to him, but those that declared that Negroes were unteachable. The words were not new to him. He had heard them before, but he had never heard them delivered with such certainty and conviction. He knew they were not true. He knew this from his own experiences and from the experiences of those closest to him, his mother and father.

Matilda and Joshua had been born in slavery and denied the benefits of a public education. Yet both had gone on to educate themselves, his father doing so while still a slave. The Negro unteachable? What of his mother and father?

In a few years he was to write a story entitled *The Ingrate*. The story recorded the adventures of his father and he named the hero Josh, a shortened version of his father's name. Josh was a slave on a plantation owned by Mr. Leckler. He was a gifted slave—the plantation plasterer—and as a result, Mr. Leckler hired him out to neighboring plantations. Josh was trying to save enough money to purchase his freedom.

The master found that it was more profitable to hire him out instead of "letting him do chores and field work in his idle time." With an eye out for profit, Leckler taught Josh to "cipher and read" so that the plantation owners would not cheat him out of his wages, most of which went to Leckler. He taught Josh for one year and, satisfied that the slave knew enough to protect his profit, demanded that he give up the idea of "book larnin." Unbeknown to the master, Josh continued to study. He read books in the morning before starting to work, at midday, and at night. One day Josh went off on a job and did not come back.

At first Leckler was not alarmed. Later, he decided to go to the employer's plantation to inquire about his slave. On arriving, he was informed that Josh had set out for home over six hours earlier. The conclusion was undisputable—Josh had run away. Later, Leckler discovered that Josh had gotten away with a pass signed by a James Leckler. The train attendant had checked the pass, noticed that it was signed in a good hand, and ushered the slave aboard. When this was reported to Leckler, he shouted hysterically at the attendant: "Forged! It was forged! He wrote it himself!"

Like Josh of *The Ingrate*, Joshua Dunbar had been a slave. He was born into bondage in Kentucky, and like the fictional character, was a plasterer who was allowed to do outside work in order to purchase his freedom. His master taught him enough to enable him to protect himself from his employers; but Joshua, not satisfied with "a little learning," continued to educate himself; he taught himself the alphabet, repeating it over and over, day after day, month after month, until finally he was able to read.

Joshua Dunbar also ran away from slavery. He did not, however, forge a pass. Aided by a friend who brought him a parting gift of "cayenne pepper," he took to the woods "on a dark and rainy night" and began to make his way to freedom. After every few steps, he spread cayenne pepper into his tracks. This was a device known to all runaway slaves. Whenever a slave was missing, the first thing the master did was to unleash a pack of bloodhounds to track the slave to his hiding place. Cayenne pepper had a heavy, pungent odor, which caused the dogs to sneeze, stop, and paw at their noses. Although not throwing them off the trail completely, this device gave the slave the much needed time to complete his escape.

Aided by a number of men—most of them Quakers—Joshua made his way to Detroit and finally crossed the border into Canada. He had escaped via "the Underground Railroad," a unique institution in American history. Its name, so the legend goes, was taken from the experiences of a slave named Tice Davids. Davids escaped from Kentucky. With his master in hot pursuit, he leaped into the Ohio River and began to swim across, pursued by his master in a row boat. When the slave owner reached the shore, the escaped man was nowhere to be found. After searching the entire area for his property, the slave owner is reported to have declared, "He must have gone on the underground railroad."

It was not a railroad in the real sense of the word, but a loose structure of many individuals, black and white, who stood watch at different "stations" along the route from South to North. When a runaway slave was entrusted to their care, they fed him, housed him, and after allowing time for recuperation, conducted him to the next station until, eventually, he reached freedom.

Once in Canada, Joshua continued his education. He worked as a plasterer during the day and studied at night. He read a great deal, and the subject that he liked best was history. He was determined to find out the true history of the black man. He read newspapers also and, in one of these, he learned of the conflict between North and South. When this conflict broke into war, Joshua decided to return and participate in the fight for the freedom of his brothers. Once in America, he wasted little time. He joined, under Colonel Norwood Penrose Hallowell of the Fifty-Fifth Massachusetts Regiment, the second regiment of black soldiers to be created in the North. Having reached the rank of sergeant, the ex-slave re-enlisted after the war. When his next tour of duty was over he left the Army and went to Dayton, Ohio, where in 1871 he married Matilda Murphy.

Like her husband, Matilda Murphy Dunbar had been a slave in Kentucky. However, the events that had brought her to Dayton were different from those that had brought Joshua. Although many women ran away during slavery, Matilda was not one of them. She was born on a plantation belonging to Squire David Glass, and when the squire died she became the property of his daughter, Mrs. Venable, of Lexington, Kentucky. She remained with the Venables until the signing of the Emancipation Proclamation. This she hailed with indescribable joy for, as she would later tell her son: "Slavery was slavery." When the Emancipation Proclamation was announced, she "sang hallelujah and jumped for joy with the other servants in the kitchen. . . ."

She did not welcome the new freedom for herself alone. Part of her joy and excitement stemmed from the knowledge that now she, her husband, and their two sons could be together. Since the age of seven, she had been hired out to different plantations to do menial chores. On one such venture, at a plantation belonging to a man whom she knew only as Mr. Murphy, she met Murphy's handyman Willis. Willis, who had taken his master's name for his own, was a sturdy, devout worker with "a great deal of tenderness and compassion." The two began a courtship that ended in marriage. Matilda Glass became Matilda Murphy and gave birth to two sons, William T. Murphy and Robert S. Murphy.

William, the first child, was born on the Murphy plantation. Shortly afterwards, Matilda was sent back to her owner. Willis could not follow. To do so would have made him a runaway slave and a fugitive from justice. The separation from her husband remained one of Matilda's most bitter memories of slavery. She once told her youngest son, Paul, "The worst part of slavery [was] that a body didn't have the say over his own life."

Neither did slaveholders have "the say" over events; and after emancipation, mother and children were reunited with husband and father. The union lasted only a short time. Like Joshua, the husband of her second marriage, Willis was also concerned about securing freedom for his people. After convincing his wife to go to Dayton and wait for him, Willis rode off to join the Union troops in post-war mopping-up operations. He died (presumably) during the course of his service.

Dayton was not an arbitrary choice, for that city had assumed importance in her life long before when Matilda was still a slave. Many curious acts took place during slavery; and none was more curious than that involving Matilda's grandmother, Aunt Becca Porter.

Becca was bought by Samuel Steele of Dayton, Ohio, who proved to be an unusual kind of abolitionist. He was not like those who were content to make "fiery speeches" from platforms and return home, patting themselves on the back for having done their utmost against slavery. Steele was a man of conviction. He believed that slavery was inhuman and immoral, and he used his money, little though it was, to buy a slave and set her free. In this way, he hoped to present an example to his fellow abolitionists. And so he bought Becca Porter, took her to Dayton, found her a place to live, got her a job, and set her free.

By the time Matilda's own mother received her freedom, her grandmother, Becca, was already settled in Dayton. Matilda's mother became free under different circumstances. As Matilda told it: "She got too old to work. At least her master thought she was too old to be much use on the plantation any more, so he set her free—free to starve, for all he knew, but that never bothered a slave owner. He just wanted to get out o' carin for slaves who couldn't break their backs for him any more."

The old woman joined Becca Porter in Dayton, and twenty years later she was followed by her daughter and her two grandchildren, who were free at last. "I found my mammy," Matilda told Paul, "and we lived in that house on Howard Street where you was born." In the house on Howard Street, Matilda began to educate herself. Her scheme for learning was ingenious. Each day she watched for children coming home from school and coaxed them into her home with cookies and milk. As payment she asked them to teach her the alphabet. When she had learned enough to read a few words, she enrolled in night school and attended until she was forced to quit in order to support her children. She could now read well enough to get through the Bible and the newspapers, and she could write well enough to keep her accounts.

Dunbar, awaiting his turn to speak at the West End Club, remembered the education of his mother and father. Chapman was saying that black people could not learn; and he was saying much more. His long speech was a pompous tirade against black people, designed to convince his audience of their unworthiness. He finished his speech. There was about him the look of a man satisfied with himself—one who, having discovered the great truth, had condescendingly passed it down to his inferiors. He bowed to the sound of polite applause, strutted from the rostrum, and began to march majestically to his seat. Halfway there he spun around as though he had been struck in the back by a cannon ball. The president had announced the next speaker. He was the "Paul Laurence Dunbar" whom Chapman had called a "freak of nature," only a few moments before. The doctor was surprised, yet he composed himself quickly, dropped into his seat and, like the rest of the audience, turned to watch the young black man stride purposefully to the rostrum.

The anger in Paul's eyes seemed to have spread to his entire face. His hands were no longer shaking; the nervousness and tenseness occasioned by rage had disappeared from his body. He was like a victorious Hannibal, fresh from combat with one enemy and in a hurry to begin combat with another. Chapman had stirred a volcano. He had brought to the surface a hideous truth which the poet himself had not wanted to acknowledge fully.

Some of his biographers have called him "the champion of his people." This was a phrase he never used in reference to himself. Although he never denied his blackness (and he could not since critics and sympathizers made the fact of his being pure black—having no admixture of white blood—one of his most important characteristics), he did not want to be known as a Negro poet, but simply as a poet. Moreover, in a book review that he later wrote Dunbar came close to arguing that blacks and whites should disappear as separate races, and become one: "While so far I have found the observable result of race blending less strong than either of the parent races, yet, I can see how the cosmopolite of the future might be the combination of the best in all the divisions of the human family—each race supplying what all the others lacked."

Like most black people in America, at times Dunbar secretly wished to be white, believing that this would enable him to escape the hardships encountered by blacks. Some black people never forsake this desire. They continue to live day after day, year after year, attempting to act like white people, as if to be black were a crime. However, when blatant attacks were made upon his race, Dunbar rose to the defense of his people with the same conviction and determination that had sent Willis Murphy and Joshua Dunbar to war against the slave system.

In similar fashion, he rose to the present situation. He felt his blackness now. Chapman's insults had gone beyond him, beyond the present race of black people; they were aimed at all members of the race—the dead as well as the unborn. Removing a copy of *Oak and Ivy* from his breast pocket, he spread it before him, opened the book to the title page, fixed his eyes coldly upon Dr. Chapman (who, having completely recovered from the shock, had assumed his previous air of pompous superiority), and announced: "I shall give you first a poem I had not intended to recite this evening when I arrived; it is called *Ode to Ethiopia*."

The audience quickly lapsed into silence. All were aware that this was Dunbar's way of drawing the battle lines.

And truly it was! Upon this platform, facing a hostile enemy, Dunbar discovered what Richard Wright was to discover many years later, "that words were weapons." "Oh Mother Race!" he began, the sound pounding into his ears, drumming out that other sound which tried to whisper from deep inside of him that it might have been better had he not been born black. He pushed this thought from his mind. The pact had been made between him and his people, and to make it secure, to leave no doubt in the minds of his white audience that he conceived of himself and his people as being inseparable, he continued:

> *O Mother Race! to thee I bring*
> *This pledge of faith unwavering,*
>   *This tribute to thy glory.*
> *I know the pangs which thou didst feel,*
> *When slavery crushed thee with its heel,*
>   *With thy dear blood all gory.*

Slavery was neither happy nor joyful; instead it was a monstrous institution that had crushed a people beneath its heels: "Sad days were those—ah, sad indeed!" Yet, from the depth of sadness, of despair, the race began its upward ascent while

> *The forests flee before their stroke*
> *Their hammers ring, their forges smoke*
> *They stir in honest labor.*

The chant of his voice kept time with the slow, rhythmic gyrations of his athletic young body as the words of the Ode pushed him on to greater heights of eloquence. He told of the path the race had trod; he told of the sacrifices it had made; he noted the injustices it had endured; he pointed out that there were soldiers who "tread the field where honor calls;" legislators whose "voices rang through Senate Halls." Of these things, he therefore intoned:

Be proud, my Race, in mind and soul;
Thy name is writ on Glory's scroll
 In characters of fire.
High 'mid the clouds of Fame's bright sky
Thy banner's blazoned folds now fly,
 And truth shall lift them higher.

Three years later Dunbar appeared before a different audience under different circumstances. When he recited his poem, *The Cornstalk Fiddle*, suddenly, as if inspired by his own voice, he broke into a dance, pirouetting across the rostrum, his feet and his hands moving in time with the words that echoed melodiously about the hall. The audience, aroused and moved by the combination of words and rhythm, broke into a chant, clapping their hands and stomping their feet as though under the spell of the poet.

But there was no hand clapping now, no foot stomping, no chanting. This audience, perhaps more than the other, had fallen captive to the eloquence of the poet. Not one head turned; not one sleeve rustled; not one body moved. He lowered his voice, lifted his head high, and conscious that the battle was over, the victory his, drove on to the final stanza of the poem, which though uttered in soft tones, came crashing like a crescendo into the ears, minds, and hearts of his listeners:

Go on and up! Our souls and eyes
Shall follow thy continuous rise;
 Our ears shall list thy story
From bards who from thy root shall spring,
And proudly tune their lyres to sing
 Of Ethiopia's glory.

II

OAK AND IVY

The serious poems were stronger than the humorous and dialect pieces.
The lesser ones were like ivy twined around a tree trunk—and there was his title: Oak and Ivy.

—JEAN GOULD

A few months later Dunbar was reciting *Ode to Ethiopia* again, but this time in Chicago rather than Toledo. On this occasion the audience consisted of only one man—the revered and respected "Negro" leader, Frederick Douglass, a former slave, an abolitionist leader, an eloquent spokesman, and gifted writer. Long before Dunbar's time, he became a hero to black men in bondage everywhere. He had already become "a growing legend," one that was to survive the years.

As applied to most men, legend is more fiction than fact. This cannot be said of Frederick Douglass; his legendary actions are more fact than fiction. Legend has it that he was an untutored slave, who was educated in part by his mistress; that when sufficiently educated he ran away to the North; that in but a short time he became one of the most distinguished of the abolitionist speakers; that he wrote three books about his life, edited four newspapers, and served as a conductor for slaves who hid out in his Rochester, New York, home. Legend does not stop there. It is said that he was friendly with old John Brown and with the black women abolitionists, Harriet Tubman and Sojourner Truth; that he influenced Presidents Lincoln, Johnson, and Grant; that he never lessened his efforts in behalf of the rights of his people. And legend did not lie one whit.

Douglass was now near the end of his remarkable career. In two years the old warrior would be dead. But here, sitting in quiet contemplation, listening to the young man recite the lines of his favorite poem, there was no inkling of his coming death. His eyes, beneath the great mane of white hair, were closed as if in prayer. The old man enjoyed the poem, but his enjoyment could not have surpassed that of the young poet who lingered upon each word of the Ode as if to prolong that historic moment. When Dunbar had decided to come to the World's Fair, he'd had no idea that one of his rewards would be meeting Frederick Douglass.

The 1893 World's Fair was held in Chicago during the summer. Many people whom Dunbar knew were going to the Fair to find work. His brother Robert already lived in Chicago, but still Dunbar hesitated. There was no guarantee that he would find work at the Fair. At least in Dayton he had his job at the Callahan Building. Besides, he would have to leave his mother. How would the mortgage be paid if he went to Chicago and didn't find work right away?

Yet, on the other hand, the separation from his mother would be short—he could send for her as soon as he had a job. In a large city like Chicago, where such an event as the "World's Columbian Exhibition" (the official name of the Fair) was to be held, finding work might not be too difficult. There was even the possibility that he might find a job making more money than he made at the Callahan Building. Then, there was the most important lure of all. The Dayton *Herald*, the first paper to publish his poems and the paper that had recently published one of his short stories, had commissioned him to write a feature story, entitled, "Dayton at the Fair."

He arrived in the "Windy City" three weeks before official opening of the Exhibition. He stayed with his brother and family while he searched for work. However, Robert's home was too small to accommodate Dunbar. After a few days, he knew that he would have to leave. Lacking his cherished privacy, he felt as if he were being stifled. The fear that would haunt him all of his life was born here: a fear of imprisonment, of the loss of freedom and movement.

He managed to get a job as a waiter in a downtown hotel, a job that paid more than he had earned running the elevator in Dayton. However, there was an even greater reward. As a result of his experiences at the hotel, he wrote one of his best dialect poems. "Seen my lady home las' night/ jump back, honey, jump back," run the lines of *A Negro Love Song*, a poem that almost reaches perfection in meter and rhythm.

There are two speakers in the poem. One is a lover, gossiping about his amorous adventures of the previous night. The other is a waiter who keeps interrupting with the refrain "jump back, honey, jump back."

The story behind the composition of the poem is as interesting as the poem itself. The hotel management hired extra waiters in expectation of a large crowd at the Fair. The waiters took turns serving the people in the dining hall, and as a result there were always a few extra waiters standing about. They stood around in small groups, gossiping about the adventures of the night before, which, more often than not, involved some romantic escapade. When the waiters who were busy came through the swinging doors, trays piled high with dishes, they would shout to the group gathered behind the door "jump back." If the first request did not spur the group to movement, the warning was given a second time, "jump back, honey, jump back." It was this situation that suggested to Dunbar the story line for his poem.

Having once begun, he worked on it for two days before satisfying himself that he had accurately portrayed the actions of both waiters and gossipers in poetical form. The poem begins:

> Seen my lady home las' night,
>   Jump back, honey, jump back.
> Hel' huh han' an' sque'z it tight,
>   Jump back, honey, jump back.
> Hyeahd huh sigh a little sigh,
> Seen a light gleam f'om huh eye,
> An' a smile go flittin' by—
>   Jump back, honey, jump back.

And on it continues. The speaker, while relating his conquest of the previous night, is constantly interrupted by the busy waiters. The poem consists of three stanzas of eight lines each with the final stanza summing up the night's adventure in suspenseful fashion:

> Put my ahm aroun' huh weys',
>   Jump back, honey, jump back.
> Raised huh lips an' took a tase,
>   Jump back, honey, jump back.
> Love me, honey, love me true?
> Love me well ez I love you?
> An' she answe'd, "Cose I do"—
>   Jump back, honey, jump back.

Two years later, in July of 1895, the poem was set to music by Will Marion Cook, soon to become famous as a composer and arranger. He also arranged for the song to be included in the score of *Clorindy, or the Origins of the Cakewalk,* the work on which he was presently working. He invited the poet to write more lyrics for his musical, but Dunbar had too many other commitments.

The Fair opened in the middle of May. Dunbar left the job in the hotel dining room and found employment on the Fair grounds. He had come to Chicago to see the Fair, and he wanted to be as close to the grounds as possible. He found a job as caretaker of a washroom in one of the Fair's main buildings. This job paid more than the hotel job. He earned more money than he had ever earned in his life—$10.50 a week, which was double what he had earned in Dayton. In addition, he worked only five hours a day. Therefore, he had time to wander about, taking in the Fair, meeting people, and making friends.

Wendell Phillips Dabney, one of his new-found friends, introduced him to young Joseph Douglass, grandson of the black leader. Through his association with Joseph, Dunbar came face to face with this man who was bigger than legend. The first meeting took place in the parlor of Wheeler's boarding house where Douglass usually took his meals. Standing before a man whose life had been filled with more drama and wonder than any poet could hope to capture, Dunbar was nervous and self-conscious.

Lately, Douglass was seldom at his best. These were the times of despair. The high hopes he had held for his country and his people were now gone. His people had not failed him, but his country had failed both him and his people. Although slavery, the most pernicious of man-made institutions, had been declared illegal, the new day that he had believed would follow its eclipse had not arrived. Moreover, now the chance that it would arrive seemed unlikely.

The consequences of the failure of Reconstruction were now being felt. Initially, there had been many victories won by the forces of justice and right: the Thirteenth, Fourteenth, and Fifteenth Amendments, and the Civil Rights Act of 1875. Of these only the Amendments remained. The Civil Rights Act of 1875 had gone further than any other measure to make the Fourteenth Amendment, which granted citizenship to the former slaves, a reality. It had prohibited segregation and discrimination in public accommodations; but the act had been declared unconstitutional by the Supreme Court in 1883. In addition to actual legislation during Reconstruction, many black men and women had sat in the state legislatures and in Congress—several had served as Lieutenant Governors, one as acting governor of a Southern state—and others had held lesser offices throughout the reconstructed states. They had now been replaced—by segregationists and race haters who used violence and perverted the law in order to accomplish their ends. With the departure of black officeholders went progressive programs in the areas of education, social welfare, and health care.

America was now turning her eyes towards industrialism and economic expansion. As a result, she saw new worlds to conquer in the South for such interests as steel, railroads, and oil. Thus, the Negro problem became less important to the North and West than it had been before. Its solution was left to the sons and daughters of the South's old master class.

More heartbreaking for Douglass was the fact that the tremendous loyalty and affection with which he had been regarded by his people had been shaken. This initially occurred when he took a white woman as his second wife, and was later reinforced when he accepted the position of Minister to Haiti. Perhaps the affection was never to really wane. But as for the loyalty, Douglass knew that this was a completely different situation. For most blacks, the journey from slavery to freedom had been a tortuous one over high, seemingly impassable precipices. It was natural that afterwards many who had taken the journey wished for an era of peace and calm. The followers were not as willing as they had once been—before the hopes of Reconstruction had been frustrated—to ride the black stallion of confrontation and agitation. This new mood would account for the acquiescence to the policies of Booker T. Washington three years later.

Despite his despair, Douglass greeted the poet affectionately. He told Dunbar that he had read of him in one of the western papers, and that he had hopes for him. Later in the evening he offered the poet a job as an assistant in the Haitian exhibit at the Fair. Although Douglass was in charge of the Haitian office, his funds were limited. Consequently, his offer was less than the young man's previous salary—five dollars a week, which the black statesman was to pay out of his own pocket. But Dunbar did not hesitate. The opportunity to work beside Frederick Douglass was worth more than the five-dollar cut in salary. He was exhilarated.

To show his appreciation, Dunbar offered Douglass a copy of *Oak and Ivy*, the book from which he had just read. The Negro leader wanted to pay for it; but Dunbar held firm, insisting that the book be accepted as a gift. Finally, Douglass relented and folded the little book under his arm. "If you give me this," he said, "I shall buy others." Dunbar met the twinkle in the old man's eye with a smile. He was one of the few people to ever win a debating point with the eloquent Frederick Douglass.

. *Oak and Ivy* had found a home in the most distinguished company during its short existence. The journey had been a splendid one. It had begun with sales to neighbors, classmates, and friends, and now it was nestled close to the bosom of the greatest living black man. A strange journey indeed. Yet the history of this volume of poems was far stranger, starting prior to 1892, the year in which the book was published.

Dunbar had still been a student at Central High School age of six, but it was at Central that he first began to publish a book of his poems. He had been writing poetry since the age of six. But it was at Central that he first began to publish regularly. Hardly an issue of the school paper was published that did not contain a contribution from his pen. In 1888, while he was still a student, the Dayton *Herald* published his poem, *Our Martyred Soldiers*, which was followed five days later by another of his poems, *On the River*. Neither of the poems was written in dialect. They were both written in standard English, as was the case with most of his early poetry. His first real attempts at creation were written in the English spoken by his mother, father, neighbors, and classmates.

"Poetry," wrote the English poet John Keats, "should come naturally or it should not come at all." Poetry came naturally to the young man from Dayton, Ohio, but not the decision to become a poet. Dunbar had entertained notions of becoming a lawyer and had gone so far as to study law in his spare time at the Callahan Building. His mother had wanted him to become a minister. He forsook both of these professions for the not-so-respectable one of poet. It is difficult to tell when he finally decided to make this his life's vocation. Throughout his life, he regretted the fact that he had not attended college. Even after the publication of *Oak and Ivy*, he still entertained the idea of taking college courses, although he was not under the illusion that college would enable him to write better poetry. One can only conjecture as to the time when the thought of devoting his life to poetry crystallized in his mind.

Perhaps it was in the summer of 1892. On June 27th of that year, the Western Association of Writers held its annual conference in Dayton at the Town Opera House. The job of finding someone to give the welcoming address was entrusted to Mrs. Helen Truesdale, an English teacher at Central High School. Mrs. Truesdale's first thought was of the young poet, whose poems had made him well known among Dayton's citizens. Three days before the opening of the conference, she sought him out at his elevator post, and invited him to give the welcoming address.

To say that he was flattered is an understatement. To be more accurate, he was overwhelmed. He was being asked to address a conference of writers from across the nation. Was this not recognition of his standing as a poet? Was there not someone else who believed as strongly in his potential as he did? How gratifying that, in all of Dayton, Mrs. Truesdale had selected him, a writer, to talk to other writers. He began to think about what he would say. Why not something different from the usual fare? He was a writer and writers were supposed to be innovative. Very well, innovate he would. He would not give his address in prose as was the usual procedure. He was a poet and he would memorialize this event by giving his address in verse.

It was not the event alone that he would memorialize. June 27th was his birthday. It was on that day twenty-two years ago that he had been born in Dayton on Howard

Street, only a few miles from the Opera House at which he was to speak. His parents had never been among the town's leading citizens. Matilda was respected, to be sure. Yet, she had to earn her living doing what she knew best—washing and ironing clothes for her neighbors. Joshua Dunbar, frustrated and insecure because of not being able to find work to support his family, had left home and taken up residence in the Old Soldiers' Home. He never returned to the house on Howard Street.

Dunbar was frail and often in ill health. Many had doubted that he would survive childhood. But he had. Despite the hardships encountered by his mother, he had survived and he was now about to do the unthinkable. The son of a washerwoman was about to address a group of distinguished scholars and writers.

The poem was very long, yet the audience sat in the sweltering heat, surprised and enthralled. He quoted from the philosopher Bishop Berkeley, spoke of the Hesperides and paid tribute to the West, all in verse. He spoke of the "art, science, and the industries" calling them "New Fruits," and assured the assembly of writers that his city, Dayton, extended a glad hand to those who ". . . tune the laureled lyre/To songs of love or deeds of fire."

And then he was gone. He bowed to the applause which was long and loud, stepped off of the stage, and hurried away. He had taken an hour off from his elevator, and the clock on the steeple told him that his time was almost up. Once back at his post, he took time to reflect on the events of the day. This had been the most exciting birthday ever. He had faced a large group of people for the first time and had not been nervous. He had recited his poem carefully, gesturing at the proper time, slowing or quickening his voice for maximum effect. Yes, he thought, the day had gone well. He wondered if the others shared his belief.

Unexpectedly, the answer arrived very soon. The next day the Callahan Building was invaded by three men. They were among the most important writers at the conference: Dr. John Clark Ridpath, Dr. James Newton Matthews, and Mr. Will Pfrimmer. They found the young poet eating lunch on a staircase near the elevator. He did not recognize them. Of the three, Dr. Ridpath was the only one to whom he had spoken at the conference, and then only briefly as Ridpath had introduced him to the audience. At first Dunbar thought they were passengers who had come to find out why the elevator was unattended.

However, these men had not come to be chauffeured to different floors but to praise him for yesterday's performance. They had found out from Mrs. Truesdale that he had written the poem which he delivered, and they congratulated him on its excellence. They also requested personal copies of this poem, and of others which he had published. They concluded by inviting him to return to the conference to read some of his poetry.

This long conversation took place between floors of the Callahan Building. They began their conversation on the ground floor, but the buzzer rang almost immediately. Dunbar excused himself, rushed off to pick up the passenger and had no sooner resumed the conversation with his three guests than the buzzer called him again. Finally, one of the guests suggested that they accompany him on his trips and the little elevator zoomed from floor to floor with its curious cargo—three white men and a black poet, engaged in serious discussion. After the elevator touched ground for about the nineteenth time, the trio departed, but not before grasping the young man's hands affectionately and reminding him of his promise to return to the conference where he was invited to join the association.

The applause that greeted Dunbar on his return was tumultuous. The entire assemblage rose as one to give him a standing ovation. They continued their show of approval as he read his poetry, some of which had been published previously, but most of which was being presented for the very first time.

At the conclusion of the conference, Dr. Matthews took him aside. "I think the world should know about you," he said. "I'm sure your work will speak for itself in time, but it won't do any harm to hasten the process with a little publicity." Dr. Matthews promised to help in directing the world's attention to the talented young man. He said he would send a letter praising "the poet" from Dayton, Ohio, to a chain of newspapers.

Shortly after his successful appearance before the Western Association of Writers' Conference, Dunbar began to think seriously about publishing a volume of his poems. He made a survey of his neighbors and former classmates who had encouraged him to undertake such a venture in the past and had implied that, if he wanted to publish his works, they would aid him. Meanwhile, Dr. Matthews kept his promise. His letter resulted in correspondence from a number of people, most of whom wanted more information about the young black poet from Dayton. Among the letters forwarded to Dunbar was one from the "Hoosier Poet," James Whitcomb Riley, the most respected poet of the day. Riley's letter was encouraging and did much to give Dunbar a sense of confidence in making the decision he was contemplating.

He still wanted a college education and sometimes he wondered if this would not be more rewarding than a career as a poet. His flirtation with the law was almost over, although at times he continued to entertain the idea of becoming a great barrister. There was also the question of the ministry. This had caused him the greatest concern, for in rejecting a career as a minister, he was rejecting his mother's fondest wish. She had decided, long ago, on a ministerial career for him. Kindly and with tact he attempted to dissuade her. He was not against religion; but as his autobiographical novel, *The Uncalled*, would show, he was opposed to the rules and restrictions that religion would impose on him. A sensitive spirit such as his craved and needed freedom in order to survive.

And thus he decided to become a poet. He came home one day and surprised his mother. She had kept newspaper clippings and magazines containing his poems in a box. He asked for these, smiling all the while. Matilda, having grown accustomed to the strange antics of her youngest son, produced the box. The pile of poems was a fair-sized one. He selected the best of these, added some new ones and turned to his inquisitive mother with the announcement that he was going to publish a book. He told her that some of the people in town had promised to help him. Matilda smiled and turned her head. She was more sophisticated than her son. She knew, even if he did not, that a wide gap lay between promise and action.

He discovered this fact soon enough. The offered help was not forthcoming. The following day, he found himself alone in the office of the United Brethren Publishing House. He was depressed, but he tried to maintain an air of composure. He asked about the possibility of publishing a book of poems. An editor informed him that the company would not finance the publication of a book of poems on a royalty basis. Poetry was not one of the products for which Americans spent large sums of money. The poems could be pub-

lished only if Dunbar paid the printing costs out of his own
pocket; the amount, the editor coldly announced, was one
hundred and twenty-five dollars.

Slowly, he turned away. He earned only four dollars a
week. One hundred and twenty-five dollars was as hard to
come by as the pot of gold at the end of the rainbow. With
his head down, he began to walk out of the building. He was
stopped near the door by the business manager, William L.
Blacher. Blacher had seen Dunbar around the city, and knew
something of his activities at Central High School. He called
the poet to his desk. "What's wrong, Paul?" he asked kindly.
Dunbar, close to tears, related the story from beginning to
end. Blacher picked up the manuscript and looked it over
carefully, rereading a few of the poems several times. He
seemed pleased with what he read. The careful appraisal
over, he announced that he would advance the one hundred and twenty-five dollars and that Dunbar could pay him
back out of the sales of copies of the book.

The poet was thrilled beyond belief. The excitement
shone in his eyes, in his dark handsome face, in his lithe
young body. The world outside was filled with sunshine and
laughter. Each face he passed was the face of a friend, the
call of each bird a sound of pleasure, the world a big round
beautiful orb of beautiful things and beautiful people. He
was going to have a book published. The book would bear
his name and contain his poetry. It would be published by
the first of January 1893.

The book was printed before Christmas, however. It was
a slender book—there were only sixty-two pages—containing fifty-six poems. In literary terms these poems were
juvenalia—the first attempts of a young man to explore the
meaning of nature and the world. As with most juvenalia,
the early poems foreshadowed the themes and conflicts

of his later works. In such poems as *October*, the poet sang to nature with the passion and enthusiasm that would increase as he grew older: "But what cares she that jewels should be lost,/When all of Nature's bounteous wealth is hers?"

Here, too, could be found the first tribute to race. Dunbar's first call to his people to "strive ever onward" was given in *Ode to Ethiopia*. Other poems hinted at what was to become the major conflict of his life. This can best be seen in *A Career*. This poem is more than juvenalia; in a sense it is almost a prophecy—the young poet seemed able to see beyond the present and capable of knowing and analyzing the future:

> *Break me my bounds, and let me fly*
> *To regions vast of boundless sky;*
> *Nor I, like piteous Daphne, be*
> *Root-bound. Ah, no! I would be free*
> *As yon same bird that in its flight*
> *Outstrips the range of mortal sight;*
> *Free as the mountain streams that gush*
> *From bubbling springs, and downward rush*
> *Across the serrate mountain's side,—*

This poem contained the plea that would echo through the few remaining years of his life: "Oh, circumscribe me not by rules/That serve to lead the minds of fools!"

Despite the importance of *A Career* to Dunbar's development as a poet, few of his biographers have realized its full implication. Had they done so, they might have noted that Dunbar's most serious poems in *Oak and Ivy* were written in standard English and that the poet himself was less than pleased with the success of his dialect pieces.

The fault does not lie entirely with the biographers. Although holding his dialect pieces in contempt, Dunbar only disavowed their worth privately or in verse. He continued to recite them in public and to produce them at the drop of a hat for cynical publishers. In *Oak and Ivy*, for example, his use of dialect poems undercuts the force of his message in *A Career*. Such poems as *The Old Apple-Tree, My Sort O' Man*, and the exceptionally bad *Goin' Back* were sellouts to the national mentality. They were poems written from personal expediency, and the high principles he had set for himself appear to have been forgotten. A few lines of *Goin' Back*, illustrate both of these points.

> *But now I'm goin' back agin,*
> *To the blue grass medders an' fiel's o' co'n*
> *In the dear ol' State whar I was bo'n. . . .*
> *Back to my ol' Kaintucky home,*
> *Back to the ol' Kaintucky sights,*
> *Back to the scene o' my youth's delights, . . .*

Dunbar never took these poems seriously. For him they were humorous ditties written to entertain white audiences. Few black people could afford to spend a dollar for his book. Therefore, he was able to sell enough copies to repay his debt three weeks after publication only because of the book's popularity with whites. They bought copies for themselves and sent others to their friends. Some, like Attorney Thatcher and Dr. Tobey, were sophisticated men who differentiated between the humorous poems and the more serious ones. As for the others, he had tried to instruct them. His title was his way of choosing between his poems in dialect and those in standard English. He thought of a tree with ivy growing all about it. The tree was more important than the ivy, for the ivy was neither strong nor functional, but merely useless ornamentation. So, too, was the ivy of his book—the dialect poems—ornamentation to the sturdy oak—the poems in standard English. Only later in life was he to learn that within this title he had planted the seeds of a truer metaphor; that of the ivy engulfing the oak, strangling the life out of it, so that in time what was at first ornament replaced the dominant element, and was admired as if it had always been the more important of the two.

III

A JINGLE IN A BROKEN TONGUE

But ah, the world, it turned to praise
A jingle in a broken tongue.

Dunbar was in Toledo again in August of 1895. During the two years that had elapsed since his first engagement at the West End Club, the scene of his earlier encounter with Dr. Chapman, he had often traveled to that city under the sponsorship of Attorney Thatcher. And the lawyer's interest in the young man had increased with time. Thatcher, who had been among those to whom Mrs. Conover had sent a copy of *Oak and Ivy*, had become convinced in the years since first meeting the poet that he was a young man of fine character, of promise, and of extremely good nature. Acting on his own, the lawyer secured promises from some of Toledo's most respected businessmen to aid Dunbar.

As a result, each contributor had promised a yearly sum which was to go towards paying for a college education at one of the best colleges—probably, Thatcher hoped, Harvard. The plan was presented to Dunbar. Once again he thought of his first ambition. The desire to go to college was still strong, but he had already decided that, whatever the cost, he would pursue his chosen career as a poet. After much soul searching, he declined the lawyer's offer, and subsequently went to Chicago.

When he returned from the World's Fair in late 1893, Dayton and the nation had been hit by a severe depression. Men were out of work. Prices were unusually high. Finding jobs was extremely difficult. He was luckier than most. The man who had taken his job at the Callahan Building decided to leave Dayton for good, and Dunbar was rehired at the same salary of four dollars a week. By selling copies of *Oak and Ivy*, he was able to supplement his salary, but not enough to make ends meet. There was barely enough money for food, hardly enough to keep up the payments on the home he had purchased after the publication of *Oak and Ivy*, and none whatsoever with which to send for his mother who had remained behind in Chicago.

He turned to his pen. Like a madman, he wrote feverishly—out of a sense of desperation. He had been promised a place on a tour with a Negro opera company, and he devoted much of his time to writing pieces for this anticipated venture. However, ten days before he was to depart he was informed that the tour had been canceled. He then turned to readings. He made trips to Detroit as well as to communities in and around Ohio, but as fast as he earned a little money he spent it for necessities. By November of 1894 his hopes had all but vanished; he was despondent, morose, and desperate. He wrote to a friend: "There is only one thing left to do, and I am too big a coward to do that."

As a last resort, he turned to his friend in Toledo. He explained the severity of his situation to the lawyer and, reminding Thatcher of his promise to help him through college, asked if he would advance him some of the money previously offered to help him out of his present difficulties. However, due to Dunbar's negative response to their previous offer of tuition, the other businessmen refused to aid him now. Thatcher stood alone. He advanced the money from his own pocket, sending it hurriedly by wire. There was enough to save the house, pay a few bills, and send for his mother. Thatcher had proven himself to be a friend in need.

But those times were behind him now. As he alighted

from the train in August of 1895 the man who was watching
for him was not Mr. Thatcher, but another of Toledo's most
respected citizens, who was also to play an important part
in Dunbar's career. He was Dr. H. A. Tobey, Superintendent
of the State Hospital for the Insane. Those who knew Tobey
well spoke of him as a fair man, one who believed that man's
greatest reward on earth was to be found in helping others.
He devoted himself to this task. He made it known that he
was interested in helping any young man, regardless of his
race or color, if the young man was motivated to move ahead
in the world. A friend called his attention to the Dayton
poet, Paul Laurence Dunbar. Tobey immediately began to
make inquiries about the poet. The reports were favorable.
Thatcher, for whom Tobey had a great deal of respect, spoke
highly of the young man from Dayton. Acquaintances of
Tobey's in Dayton commented enthusiastically on the poet's
character and integrity.

In a few months Tobey had found out a great deal about
Dunbar. He knew that the poet was nearly poverty-stricken,
that he was attempting to purchase a home for his mother,
that he was trying to make something of himself as a writer,
and that he was doing all of this while working long hours
each day running an elevator. He had read *Oak and Ivy,* but
had been unable to find much of merit in it. After his inquiries he read it a second time and found a meaning in the
poems that had escaped him before. He was now convinced
that Dunbar was the kind of young man who was deserving
of help. In July he wrote Dunbar a letter, the following lines
of which stand out from all the others: "I have talked with
a number of friends of mine and believe I am in a position
to give you financial aid if you desire to increase your education or to travel with a view of better qualifying yourself to
pour out your poetical songs to the world. . . ."

". . . pour out your poetical songs to the world." The poet was to receive many letters during his career, but none would be more satisfying than this one. Tobey had read the poems in standard English as well as those in dialect. However, it was not the poems in dialect to which he was referring. He had taken note of the pieces in standard English, had liked them, and praised them. He ended his letter with: "What we need is more persons to interpret Nature and Nature's God. I believe you are especially endowed for this work . . ." The letter contained a check and a request for several copies of *Oak and Ivy*.

The check enabled Dunbar to attend another meeting of the Western Association of Writers, held in July of 1895. Three days after receiving Tobey's letter and one day after his return from the meeting, Dunbar answered the doctor's letter. His response began innocently enough. Dunbar thanked Tobey for the letter and the check, pointed out his recent hardships, stated his determination to make something of himself and mentioned the willing sacrifices he made on behalf of his mother. However, two paragraphs before the end, he wrote this revealing passage: "Your informant [referring to an inquiry made by Tobey about the poet in Dayton] was mistaken as to my aspirations. I did once want to be a lawyer, but that ambition has long since died out before the all-absorbing desire to be a worthy singer of the songs of God and Nature. To be able to interpret my own people through song and story, and to prove that after all we are more human than African."

The phrase "more human than African" is not merely figurative language used to decorate a long sentence. The sentence is a fragment and is unnecessary to the rest of the passage or to the rest of the letter. The phrase was not added to appeal to Tobey's prejudices, for Dunbar did not know the doctor and could have no idea as to what they might be. However, the phrase reveals a great deal about Dunbar as well as about the country in which he lived.

The institution of slavery in America was the worst in recorded history. This was not solely because of the brutality with which the slaves were treated. Other countries had treated their slaves equally as brutally, but no other country had sought to destroy so completely the slave's conception of his former homeland. When Africans were brought to America they were separated from one another. No two slaves who spoke the same language or belonged to the same tribe were to be sold together. All that the African had known and loved in Africa was taken from him. He was forced to learn a new language, a new culture, and to create a new self-image for himself and his children.

To do this he was taught to despise his old image, to hate his motherland. Many had noble blood flowing in their veins, yet they too were taught that Africa, their homeland, was a jungle inhabited by half men; that they themselves were savages who had fed on human flesh, run naked in the woods, and committed such acts as devouring their own young. How successful this attempt at brainwashing was can be seen in the poetry of Phillis Wheatley, a slave girl from Africa, brought to America while still quite young:

> *Father of mercy, 'twas thy gracious hand*
> *Brought me in safety from those dark abodes.*

The "dark abode," the dark continent, forbidding—Africa became known in these terms to the children of her former citizens. During Dunbar's lifetime, this myth about Africa and her people was believed by men of all races and colors, in every walk of life, throughout America. Africa was written of in derogatory terms in history books, text books, novels, and poems. The newly freed Afro-Americans, struggling for a place in the sun, were willing to sacrifice their heritage for the honor of being known as Americans. They took part in the making of myths and the distortion of African culture. "What is Africa to me?" sang Countee Cullen in the twentieth century. Few black men of Dunbar's generation ever pondered the question. To most of them Africa was the homeland which had to be civilized by black and white missionaries or forgotten altogether.

Dunbar would rather have forgotten it. He was increasingly falling under the sway of tradition and convention. He truly desired to "interpret the souls of my people"; yet he was cynically aware that he was not doing so. The poet whom Thatcher had met in 1893 was a changed man. Despite his financial condition, the name of Paul Laurence Dunbar was growing more and more familiar. His works had been published in many newspapers and magazines, including the New York *Times*, the *Chicago Magazine*, *Munsey's*, *Blue and Grey*, and *The Independent*. More important, *The Century*, one of the country's best journals, had accepted three poems, *Love-Song*, *Curtain* and *The Dilettante*, which were to be featured, wrote the editor, in a section entitled, "In the Lighter Vein."

Dunbar was not pleased with this designation for his poems; yet, instead of making his displeasure known, he only confided it privately to a few friends. Humorous and dialect poetry paid. It was what the editors wanted. One had confided to him at the Chicago World's Fair, "I'll take anything you write in dialect." And so he wrote dialect. More and more. Much of his new work was in the dialect vein. This decision was not made solely in the interest of making a quick profit. Most of his biographers have attributed to him a sophistication that he did not possess. He was, in reality, a small-town Midwesterner in thought and outlook. This accounts in part for his animosity towards the big city. He was incapable of divining the sinister forces at work in the society; and he believed that once he had established himself as a poet through the medium of dialect, his white audience would accept whatever he offered in a poetical vein. He later confessed to James Weldon Johnson: "You know, of course, that I didn't start as a dialect poet. I simply came to the conclusion that I could write it as well, if not better than anybody else I knew of, and that by doing so I should gain a hearing. I gained the hearing, and now they don't want me to write anything but dialect."

Not all of his poetry during this period was written in a humorous vein or in dialect. In April of 1895, he was called upon to write a memorial ode. Frederick Douglass had passed away that February, and when Dunbar began to write about the fallen leader, the tears occasionally blotted out his words on the paper, leaving dark streaks where words should have been. There was no need to cater to public taste in this project. The ode to his idol was not written for *The Century* or the New York *Times.* The poem was written for millions of black men who, figuratively, were the children of Frederick Douglass. But even more, the ode was in part directed to the poet himself. The message was a reminder that he should always be aware of the difference between illusion and reality; that he should never lose sight of the disparity between being a poet and being an entertainer. For white people, he was forced to be an entertainer; black people demanded a poet.

The contrast between himself and Douglass is pointed up in the fourth stanza of the ode:

And he was no soft-tongued apologist;
He spoke straightforward, fearlessly uncowed;
The sunlight of his truth dispelled the mist,
And set in bold relief each dark hued cloud;
When men maligned him, and their torrent wrath
In furious imprecations o'er him broke
He kept his counsel as he kept his path;
'Twas for his race, not for himself he spoke.

In the next to the last stanza, he cried out from the soul of his race and from the depths of his own personal anguish:

We weep for him, but we have touched his hand,
And felt the magic of his presence nigh,
The current that he sent throughout the land,
The kindling spirit of his battlecry.
O'er all that holds us we shall triumph yet,
And place our banner where his hopes were set!

But by August of 1895 the mourning period was behind him. He stepped from the railroad at the Toledo depot and was met by two men. One, a white man with blue eyes and a curly mustache, was Dr. Tobey. The other, a black man, was Charles Cottrill, an acquaintance of the doctor's who had been persuaded to come and help smooth over the meeting between Tobey and Dunbar. Cottrill stayed in the background. He pondered the remark Tobey had made as Dunbar stepped from the carriage. "Thank God, he's black," Tobey had observed. "Whatever genius he may have cannot be attributed to the white blood he may have in his veins."

Cottrill knew the reasons for this remark as well as the sentiment that lay behind it. In writing of Phillis Wheatley, Thomas Jefferson had made disparaging remarks about her ability as a poet and had followed these remarks with an attack upon the entire race. No member of the black race, he argued, had ever contributed anything meaningful to civilization. (Somewhat embarrassed by a letter from Benjamin Banneker, the black scientist whose work proved the contrary, Jefferson later made a partial retraction.)

Other racists pushed Jefferson's thesis further. No black throughout history, who did not have white blood in his veins, the emendation went, had ever contributed to the making of civilization. This myth was quite prevalent in the nineteenth century, and it was to this that Dr. Tobey was alluding. The same point was echoed by Dunbar's friends, critics, and biographers. His "pure black skin" became as great an attraction as his dialect poetry. For some unscrupulous supporters and for many in his white audience, the two seemed to go hand in hand.

Dunbar's reading for the staff and inmates of the sanitorium was very well received. Among the works which he read was one of his best dialect poems, *When Malindy Sings*. The reader must be careful not to miss the irony in this poem in which a black servant mocks the singing of her white mistress, which can be heard throughout the house. The servant compares the mistress' singing to that of the black Malindy, and Malindy comes off the better of the two. Part of the final line, usually sung by the poet whenever he recited it, was the title of a Negro spiritual, "Swing Low, Sweet Chariot"—a favorite song of depressed slaves.

Dunbar spent two days with Tobey and his family. He made new friends, among them Samuel "Golden Rule" Taylor, Mayor of Toledo, and Brand Whitlock, later U. S. Ambassador to Belgium. They were all impressed with the young man from Dayton and equally determined to aid him in his career. Like Thatcher, Dr. Tobey brought up the subject of a college education, and Dunbar rejected it on the same grounds that he had previously rejected Thatcher's proposal.

However, Tobey was not a man who was easily dissuaded. After Dunbar had returned to Dayton, Tobey sought out Attorney Thatcher. The two benefactors worked out a plan that was to be more important to Dunbar than three college scholarships. They decided to sponsor another book of his poems. The profits would belong to the poet; their reward was to come from bringing the work before the public. A man of action, Tobey moved swiftly. He consulted the firm of Hadley and Hadley, sounding them out about the prospects of printing the book. Afterwards, he wrote the poet to inform him of the arrangement.

Dunbar hurried to Toledo to give his consent in person, and the operation was soon going full blast. Tobey and Thatcher attended to the business arrangements. Dunbar rushed back to Dayton to make selections from among the new poems and those previously published in *Oak and Ivy*. The three-man team of Tobey, Thatcher, and Dunbar impressed upon Hadley and Hadley the fact that they desired publication before Christmas 1895.

Although the date of publication on the flyleaf read 1895, the book was not released until January 1896. Only Tobey, the man of action, had seen the book before the general public. Unable to wait for its release, he went to the publishing company, picked out some of the loose sheets before the book had been bound, and cut them himself. Like *Oak and Ivy*, this book was dedicated "To my mother," and only one imperfection was evidenced: the name on the title page read "Paul Lawrence Dunbar" instead of "Paul Laurence Dunbar."

In other respects the book was an improvement over *Oak and Ivy*. There were one hundred and forty-eight pages in *Majors and Minors*—more than twice the number in *Oak and Ivy*. There were seventy-four poems in the second book, an increase of eighteen over the first. Of these seventy-four poems only eleven had previously appeared in *Oak and Ivy*. Once again, the poems in standard English dominated the book. Of the seventy-four, only twenty-six were in dialect, and these were placed in a special section entitled "Humour and Dialect." The title *Majors and Minors,* like the title *Oak and Ivy,* was meant to be a guideline for his readers.

Perhaps they would see, as he did, that the term majors, meant to designate the selections he considered serious works of art, reported, however subtly, the truth that burned with such volcanic fury within his breast. Perhaps they would feel something of the agony of spirit and mind suffered by those who were forced, as in the poem *We Wear the Mask*, to ". . . smile, [while] O Great Christ, our cries/ to thee from tortured Souls arise." Perhaps they could understand his veiled plea for sympathy in the *Poet and His Song:*

> *There are no ears to hear my lays,*
> *No lips to lift a word of praise.*
> *But still, with faith unfaltering,*
> *I live and laugh and love and sing.*
> *What matters yon unheeding throng?*
>   *They cannot feel my spirit's spell,*
> *Since life is sweet and love is long,*
>   *I sing my song, and all is well.*

Perhaps they were sophisticated enough to search for the deep meaning beneath such lines as the ". . . sun, unkindly hot/My Garden makes a desert spot," or "blight upon the tree" which "Takes all my fruit away from me" so that "with throes of bitter pain/Rebellious passions rise and swell." Were there not readers whose souls were in tune with his? Could they mistake the despondent tones of *Ere Sleep Comes Down to Soothe the Weary Eyes* as an elegy for physical instead of creative death—that death of artistic sensibility, more meaningful to the poet than physical death:

> *When sleep comes down to seal the weary eyes,*
>   *The last dear sleep whose soft embrace is balm,*
> *And whom sad sorrow teaches us to prize*
>   *For kissing all our passions into calm,*
> *Ah, then, no more we heed the sad world's cries,*
>   *Or seek to probe th' eternal mystery,*
> *Or fret our souls at long-withheld replies,*
>   *At glooms through which our visions cannot see,*
> *When sleep comes down to soothe the weary eyes.*

But the world did not understand. It turned its attention to the minors—the humorous and dialect pieces—and, because of them, made the poet famous. *The Party, A Banjo Song, When De Co'n Pone's Hot,* and *The Deserted Plantation,* among others, became the overnight favorites of his readers. These poems received the heartiest applause during readings, while those "of deeper note" were accorded only polite, condescending recognition. Whatever his personal pain, whatever his private conflict, they were unimportant as long as he produced lines such as those from *A Banjo Song,* which spoke not of pain or conflict, but of contentment and joy:

Oh, dere's lots o' keer an' trouble
   In dis world to swaller down;
An' ol' Sorrer's purty lively
   In her way o' gittin' roun'.
Yet dere's times when I furgit em,—
   Aches an' pains an' troubles all,—
An' it's when I tek at ebenin'
   My ol' banjo f'om de wall.

The banjo was a symbol that everyone understood. Like the genie's magic carpet or the witch's broom, it was capable of transporting one from the reality of the present to the land of fantasy. With it one could escape into a world where there was little conflict or hatred, where black people were not a problem, but a disguised blessing. Is it any wonder that the audience asked with the narrator in *The Deserted Plantation:*

Whah's de da'kies, dem dat used to be a-dancin'
   Evry night befo' de ole cabin do'?
Whah's de chillun, dem dat used to be a-prancin'
   Er a-rollin' in de san'er on de flo'?
Whah's ole Uncle Mordecai an' Uncle Aaron?
Whah's Aunt Doshy, Sam an' Kit, an' all de res'?

The audience understood the poem's narrator better than they would understand its creator; for they were moved by the nostalgic tones and hypnotized by the "admissions":

Dey have lef' de ole plantation to de swallers,
   But it hol's in me a lover till de las';
Fu' I fin' hyeah in de memory dat follers
   All dat loved me an' dat I loved in de pas'.

This was the age of hypnotism. In comparison with Booker T. Washington, the master hypnotist, Dunbar was inconsequential. His audience was still very small; both his reading public and those whom he reached by recitals were mostly residents of the Midwest. However, Booker T. Washington had a wide audience—a national audience—and his message soothed the national conscience in a way that ten thousand *Banjo Songs* could not have done.

Nine months after Douglass' death and three months before the publication of *Majors and Minors*, Booker T. Washington had exploded upon the national scene. In October of 1895, he attended the Cotton States Exposition in Atlanta, Georgia, where he unveiled his plan for the solution of "the Negro problem." The plan was calculated to soothe the American conscience. Shrewd, political, and diplomatic, he offered nostrums for the North as well as the South, for blacks as well as whites: "To those of my race who depend on bettering their condition in a foreign land . . . I would say: 'Cast down your bucket where you are . . . Cast it down in agriculture, mechanics, in commerce, in domestic service, and in the professions.' Our greatest danger is that in the great leap from slavery to freedom we may overlook the fact that the masses of us are to live by the productions of our hands, and fail to keep in mind that we shall prosper in proportion as we learn to dignify and glorify common labor . . . No race can prosper till it learns that there is as much dignity in tilling a field as in writing a poem. To those of the white race . . . I would repeat what I say to my own race . . . 'Casting down your bucket among my people, helping and encouraging them as you are doing on these grounds, . . . you can be sure in the future as in the past, that you and your families will be surrounded by the most patient, faithful, law-abiding and unresentful people that the world has seen. As we have proved our loyalty to you in the past, in nursing your children, watching by the sick bed of your mothers and fathers, and often following them with tear-dimmed eyes to their graves, so in the future, in our humble way, we shall stand by you with a devotion that no foreigner can approach.'"

The Exposition speech should be read in its entirety for a fair assessment of the man and his policies. From the artist's point of view, it was more in the tradition of plantation literature than most of the poems and novels of the plantation school of writers. Washington also spoke of the good old days; and he held out to his audience the hope of a future in which peace would be restored and a loving, loyal, servile black race would stand ready to serve its superiors.

The nation had wanted such a speech, and it praised the man who delivered it. Overnight he became the most powerful black man in America, wielding power as no black man had ever done before—or since. "*The New York World* called him the 'Negro Moses,'" wrote Saunders Redding, "and so he proved almost to be. He was the umpire in all important appointments of Negroes; the channel through which philanthrophy flowed, or did not flow to Negro institutions; the creator and destroyer of careers; the maker and breaker of men. . . . He was appealed to on any and every subject; how many bathrooms to put in a Y.M.C.A., whether or not to start a day nursery in some town, and so on."

If he was not a "Negro Moses," he at least came close to being a black pied piper; and in no time at all, he had seized the reins of Negro leadership. In this capacity he managed to soothe not only the troubled waters, but troubled breasts as well. For trouble there was. In the year that he delivered his address in Atlanta, South Carolina successfully deprived blacks of the vote. Mississippi and Louisiana had already done so, thus establishing a pattern that was followed by each of the Reconstruction states.

Less than fifteen years before, the Supreme Court had ruled against the Civil Rights Act of 1875, thus legalizing segregation throughout the nation. One year later, in the case of Plessy *versus* Ferguson, the Supreme Court sustained segregation and upheld the doctrine of "separate but equal." More important, even as Booker T. Washington issued his assurances from the speaker's stand at the Exposition, throughout the nation black men and women were being lynched. The total number of such deaths for one year was a staggering 255. Is it any wonder that near the end of his life Frederick Douglass had begun to despair?

If Washington despaired, he did not show it. He was impressed with his own importance and he wallowed in praise like a water buffalo bathing himself after a long day on dry land. Whites across the nation accepted him as a divine prophet; those blacks who did not accept him as a leader were either silent, avoiding confrontation or inconsequential. Truth had been dethroned and Washingtonism was king.

Dunbar was one of the blacks who remained silent. In any event, at this point his opposition would have been fruitless, for he was scarcely known outside of Ohio. To friends, he confidentially voiced his disagreement with Washington's educational program, yet he did not attack Washington's overall philosophy.

The dialect poems in *Majors and Minors* were written in "the spirit which the nation needed." Although disheartened by the acclaim they continued to receive from his audiences, Dunbar continued to recite them with more consistency—if not more gusto—at each new engagement. He did not know how infectious the disease of Washingtonism was; he did not realize how similar his portrait of "the good old days" was to Washington's, nor that both portraits seemed, at times, to have come from the same brush. The philosophy of Booker T. Washington was now allied with tradition, and whatever ideas of escaping the shackles of tradition Dunbar had previously entertained were now impossible. He was trapped in a situation from which he would never be able to extricate himself.

After the publication of *Majors and Minors*, Dunbar was more concerned with personal dignity than loss of freedom. At Dr. Tobey's suggestion, he made several trips to Toledo to sell his book. To aid him in this enterprise, the doctor turned over the list of hospital supporters; but Dunbar discovered that he was a poor salesman. He was especially bashful with people whom he did not know. More than once he vowed that he would never try to sell another book. However, this mood usually passed and, days later, he could be found ringing doorbells and calling on Tobey's friends, of whom there seemed to be an endless supply.

Tobey continued to push the poet, and it was due to his prodding that Dunbar left a copy of *Majors and Minors* at the hotel of the actor-playwright James A. Herne. Herne's play, *Shores Acre*, was making a nightly run in Toledo. Dunbar, who had seen the play, advised Tobey to do likewise. Tobey was not interested in the play, but his eyes lit up at the mention of Herne's name. Why not make Herne a gift of a copy of *Majors and Minors?*

Dunbar shuddered at the idea. He did not believe that a famous playwright would see him, let alone accept a book from him. Tobey continued to push and Dunbar finally relented. He went to Herne's hotel, the Boody House, only to find that the playwright had moved to the Waldorf. There the clerk was intentionally cold. Looking at Dunbar with the contempt usually reserved for lower animals, the clerk informed him in a gruff, insulting voice that Mr. Herne was out.

Dunbar went back to the Boody House where the clerk, a friend of Tobey's, proved to be more courteous and receptive. He undertook the responsibility of seeing that the book was delivered to the actor. Dunbar left the hotel, but still was not sure that Herne would ever receive the book. He left Toledo without hearing from the actor.

Two days after his return to Dayton, he received a letter from Herne, which read in part: "While at Toledo a copy of your poems was left at my hotel by a Mr. Childs. I tried very hard to find Mr. Childs to learn more of you. Your poems are wonderful. I shall acquaint William Dean Howells and other literary people with them."

William Dean Howells! America's most famous and respected critic. Yet, once again, Dunbar entertained doubts. Why would such an important literary figure read his poems? And if he did, what good would it do? Certainly a man of his importance read many volumes of poetry each year, from men better known and established than he. He refused to allow himself to hope. He put the letter away and went off on a speaking tour, returning on June 27, his twenty-fourth birthday. Among his mail he found a hurriedly scribbled note from Tobey: "Get a copy of *Harpers Weekly* and read what William Dean Howells has to say about you."

The copy of *Harpers* was hard to come by. The current issue was devoted to the 1896 Republican Convention and highlighted the news of McKinley's nomination. Most of the newsstands were sold out, but Dunbar continued to search. Finally, after much walking, he found an issue. He paid for the magazine and, still standing in front of the news-stand, turned to the section "Life And Letters" which bore Howells' signature and read the article about himself.

He was exhilarated. This was a momentous occasion; a birthday gift beyond his wildest expectations. The most powerful critic in America had given him his blessing; had wrapped about him the cloak of importance. Howells had praised him with the words: "I do not remember any English speaking Negro . . . who has till now done in verse work of at all the same moment as Paul Laurence Dunbar, the author of the volume I am speaking of." The oracle had spoken. His tone was forceful and majestic. It was due to this oracle that Paul Laurence Dunbar went to bed one night and awoke to find himself famous.

IV

WHEN LOVE WAS YOUNG

So far from sweet real things my thoughts had strayed,
I had forgot wide fields, and clear brown streams;
The perfect loveliness that God has made,—
Wild violets shy and Heaven-mounting dreams.
And now—unwittingly, you've made me dream
Of violets, and my soul's forgotten gleam.
—Alice Dunbar Nelson

One year after Howells' review, the former elevator boy stood on the threshold of literary success. Fame and fortune seemed to be outdoing each other in vying for his attention. The world held wonders, which were beyond his ability to imagine. With Howells' help, he acquired a literary agent, Major James B. Pond, who had handled the lecture arrangements for Frederick Douglass and Mark Twain, among others. Through Pond he met several publishers, who, after Howells' review, were anxious to publish his works.

Of the three major companies interested in his work—Harper, Appleton, and Dodd, Mead—the latter made the most impressive offer. According to his contract with Dodd, Mead for his first book, Dunbar would receive "four hundred dollars advance against royalties of fifteen percent on the first 10,000 copies and 17½ percent on all sales beyond that." The book was *Lyrics of Lowly Life*—the first fruits of what were to be his harvest years.

By 1896, the world of the poet's fantasy had been transformed into a miraculous world of indescribable wonders. It was almost as if he were Cinderella, awakening to find that the glass slipper did hold magical powers; as if there were an Aladdin's lamp that could transport one to a new and different world. The *Sunday Journal* of New York City ran a feature article on him; other New York papers discovered the prose writer in the poet and published some of his fiction. Among these were the *Tribune,* the *World* and the *Sun.* An English publisher expressed interest in *Lyrics of Lowly Life* and wanted to publish an edition in England. Requests for readings flooded his Dayton home. *Lyrics of Lowly Life* was released in the summer and became an immediate best seller. Most important of all was the impressive yacht, the S.S. *Umbria,* which stood in New York harbor. The boat, which carried passengers from America to Europe, was about to embark for England. America's most famous black poet, Paul Laurence Dunbar, was to be one of its passengers.

He stood in the New York drawing room of Mrs. Victoria Earle Matthews. She was only one of a number of influential friends whom he was acquiring almost daily. She had given a reception in his honor—a ceremony befitting a monarch. There were many prominent guests from every avenue of "respectable society." One of the most important was Booker T. Washington. Yet the poet seemed sad. He greeted the guests warmly, thanked them for their fond wishes concerning his coming travels, engaged in small talk with the near-great and the great; and, yet the sadness that crept into his eyes whenever he was despondent was now discernible to those who knew him well. He stood in the midst of gaiety, surrounded by opulence and splendor—and yet, he would have given all of it away for one moment alone with a girl named Alice.

Only a short while ago he had sung in verse: "Know you, winds that blow your course/Down the verdant valleys/

That somewhere you must, perforce,/Kiss the brow of Alice?" Dunbar had never kissed either Alice or her brow; in fact, he had never been close to her, had never even seen her. There was a photograph. There were poems she had written. There were letters they had exchanged. From these he had constructed his dreams of her and had fallen in love. They were both poets and theirs was a poet's romance. Perhaps only two poets could have brought it off so well.

For Dunbar, the romance began with a poem in the *Boston Monthly Review*. One day in 1895, while looking over the magazine, he discovered the poem tucked away in one of the center pages under the byline Alice Ruth Moore. There was a face beneath the name—the face of a young girl with dark eyes and a small upturned nose. Perhaps none would call her beautiful, but few would hesitate to call her very pleasing. He read and reread the poem, pausing often to stare at the wide, dark, sensitive eyes—intelligent eyes that seemed to peer quizzically at him from the magazine page. He wrote a letter to the woman behind the photograph, praising her poem and asking for information about her and her work.

Ten days passed before he received a reply. In the meantime, he had accepted a temporary job as editor of a Negro newspaper in Indianapolis. The letter's opening lines explained the reason for the delay: "Dear Sir: Your letter was handed to me at a singularly inopportune moment—the house was on fire." The fire that had ignited the house was soon extinguished; that which had ignited the poet was just beginning to roar.

Alice Ruth Moore was born in New Orleans, Louisiana. Her parents were solidly middle class and, as Dunbar was to discover later, very proud and snobbish. She was educated in the best of schools and had gone directly to college from high school. She attended Straight College in Louisiana, the University of Pennsylvania, and Cornell University. Although she was never to become as famous as her husband, her poetry exhibits many of the characteristics of Dunbar's best verse—a sensitive appreciation of nature, a preoccupation with details, and deeply ingrained romantic tendencies. However, her strength lay, not in poetry, but in essays.

She handled this genre much better than Dunbar and as well as any of her contemporaries with the exception of W. E. B. Du Bois. One such essay, a biographical sketch of her husband written after his death, surpasses most of the full-length biographies of his life in terms of richness of content and concreteness of style. The essay, which she entitled "The Poet and His Song," reveals almost as much about the writer as it does about her subject. "Your true poet," she wrote, "is a child of nature and lies close to the motherheart. Even though he were born in the city, where his outlook on trees and fields is an incidental and sporadic occurrence in his life, he senses the divine heart pulsing beneath all things, and when he is finally brought face to face with the wonders of out-of-doors, untouched by the desecrating hand of man, he bursts into song, released from the conventionalities of other men's verse."

The romance continued through the mail. The letters became more frequent, and Dunbar more passionate. He had discovered a jewel, and like the man whom fortune befriends for the first time, he was anxious to inform the world of his find. He wrote poems to her and about her; one of these, a poem that depicts Alice as an ancient heroine, he entitled *Phyllis*. He told his mother about her; he told Tobey; Mrs. Matthews had been in on the secret for some time.

And Alice? There was something stirring inside her breast. Call it infatuation, call it love; she only knew and cared that it was there. She was inspired; captivated by his poetry. Never mind those "jingles in a broken tongue," those burlesque lines written out of desperation. It was not these that caught her eye; not these whose rhythm and message had found their way to her heart. She was attracted by the poems that sang of earth and love—young earth, young love. These were the poems that had enabled her, a poet, to love the poet in another.

Dunbar's letters became bolder. He had to see her. A way had to be found for them to get together. One poet had to meet the other. He had come to believe that such a meeting was crucial. He kept her informed of each rise in his fortunes. As more and more of his work was accepted for publication, it was as if she were a party to his every action. He imagined her peering over his shoulders as he read Howells' review, reciting aloud with him from the first copies of *Lyrics of Lowly Life,* and sitting by his side as he received praise from magazine editors of the stature of Richard Gilder of *The Century.*

Now that a trip across the ocean lay ahead, he asked himself daily why could not the spirit become flesh? The answer was obvious. The obstacles in their path were her parents, Joseph and Patricia Moore. They had successfully kept the two lovers apart for over a year. That Alice dabbled in poetry and wrote "quaint little stories" was one thing; that she might entertain ideas of marrying a poet was another. They forced Alice to cancel one meeting and vowed to forestall any others.

Mrs. Matthews drew him away from his guests; he had been talking disinterestedly, attempting to raise his voice above the music. Couples glided by on the dance floor, emitting gay laughter as they passed, the women sometimes waving a handkerchief at him. He bent his ear to the old matron's voice. Suddenly he jerked upright; his eyes and mouth widened simultaneously; he turned this way and that, looking wildly in all directions.

And then, the picture and the woman became one. Alice moved towards him, curtsied, and took his hand. Her voice was soft and melodic: "I ran away; I couldn't help it." He tried to reply, to say something with his hands. The shock of seeing her at last had paralyzed him.

Finally, he found his voice. By that time she was gone; a young man had carried her off to the dance floor. They were not reunited until the end of the party.

They went off together; away from the eyes and ears of the departing guests. They would never again, the poet vowed, be separated for so long. No, for she must marry him. In a little alcove, on the first night he had ever laid eyes on her, he proposed. And she—who had never seen him before—accepted. He took off his mother's wedding ring, which Matilda had given him long ago, and slipped it on her finger. The long night of waiting was almost over. They were engaged. Despite everything, they were engaged. Halfway to England, Dunbar wrote his mother: "You will be surprised to hear that Alice Ruth Moore ran away from Boston to bid me goodby. She took everybody by storm. . . . She is the brightest and sweetest little girl I ever met, and I hope you will not think it silly, but Alice and I are engaged. You know that is what I have wanted for two years."

Miss Edith Pond, the daughter of Major James B. Pond, accompanied Dunbar to England. She was employed to take care of his business arrangements, set up lecture engagements, and introduce him to the right people. She was a morose, short-tempered woman. She warned him, shortly before the boat left New York, that if business proved to be unprofitable, the chances were that he might have to swim home. Later, he recalled how nearly accurate her prophecy—or threat—had been.

Now, however, there was England to be considered. That country, in what may have been an attempt to purge itself of the reputation it had earned as a major participant in the slave trade, had welcomed a number of black men to its shores in the past. To England at one time or another had come Frederick Douglass; William Wells Brown, the first black man in America to write a novel; Phillis Wheatley; Henry Highland Garnet, the militant minister; and Alexander Crummell, the great educator.

London was very impressive. Of course, there was the fog, but through the dense gray haze he could make out the old buildings along Trafalgar Square, the unique shops and stores located on narrow curving streets, and the world-renowned Tower of London. England welcomed him with the same generosity it had offered his black fellow countrymen. She turned out her most learned and distinguished men to meet and hear him. At every recital one could find an assortment of explorers, writers, sculptors, musicians, scientists, and industrialists. He became, as he wrote to his mother, "the most interviewed man in England," and the claim was justified. He was to England now what the black abolitionist had been in the middle of the nineteenth century—the symbol of the black man's struggle in America.

He had neither, like William Wells Brown, crossed the ocean to raise money for the fight for freedom, nor, like others, to escape from the far-reaching arms of slave owners. However, like those who preceeded him, he was also black; in fact he was blacker than most of them. He belonged to a race of people that was, then as now, in the unenviable position of being the underdog. The English attributed their kindness to him, and to the others, to the British spirit of fair play. Yet, at the very moment they were lionizing him their missionaries were raping the continent of Africa. To be accurate, the English regarded him as, in Dr. Chapman's words, "a freak of nature."

"I do not think one can read his Negro pieces without feeling that they are of like impulse and inspiration with the work of Burns," William Dean Howells had written in his review in *Harpers*, and thousands of England's most important people came to view this "Black Burns." Like the American public, they, too, were enamored of his dialect pieces, amused by his repertoire of strange people, strange musical instruments, and strange foods, all of which appeared in his dialect poems. Explaining the unfamiliar dish mentioned in the poem, *When De Co'n Pon's Hot*, a gentleman at one of the receptions announced assuredly from the speaker's stand that "The con pone is a peculiar American dish in which the southern Negroes bake their cakes."

Dunbar was exceedingly popular. One reason for his popularity was pointed out in the cablegram an American correspondent sent to his paper. "Paul Dunbar, the Negro poet who owes to William Dean Howells his introduction to the public, is being lionized in London in the most flattering fashion. The color line is not drawn in English society, and the colored versifier, being the latest literary novelty, is much sought for receptions, garden parties, and similar gatherings."

The novelty soon wore off. Having paid their tribute to primitivism, the English turned to other things. The invitations to "receptions, garden parties, recitals and similar gatherings" which he had previously received in such large numbers slowed to a trickle and finally stopped altogether. His popularity waned; he was no longer in demand and Miss Pond, true to her word, left him in a dingy room, which he later memorialized in a poem called *The Garret*, to swim back to America if possible. Alone for the first time since the Howells' review, he began to go over the events of the last year and to attempt to place them in proper perspective.

"One critic," he wrote to a friend, "says a thing and the rest hasten to say the thing, in many cases using the identical words. I see now very clearly that Mr. Howells has done me irrevocable harm in the dictum he laid down regarding my dialect verse." The phrase "irrevocable harm" was an important admission. For the first time he became conscious of the trap that had closed about him, of the shackles placed on his freedom as a poet. He had not wanted to be a Negro poet; but he had not wanted to be a dialect poet either. Now, irrevocably, the appellation stuck to him as if grafted on by a mad scientist. He knew that the dialect tradition had been born of the most sinister of all jokes, and that as the greatest exponent of it he was the King of Jesters.

He was not the first poet to write Negro dialect. The first was a white man, Irvin Russell, whose sentiments, if not his bad poetry, Dunbar copied almost completely. Nor had he been the first black man to write Negro dialect. James Campbell, whom he had met at the Chicago Exposition, had written dialect poetry before him. However, Campbell had been unable to get a hearing. This was due partly to the fact that he lacked the artistic skill of Dunbar; but also because, as James Weldon Johnson noted, "he was free from the sweetness of the plantation tradition. His tone is generally firm."

Johnson meant that Campbell's verse was more representative of the minstrel tradition than the plantation. The objective of the minstrel tradition was to make white people laugh, to serve as a diversionary force. If the black man was regarded as a clown, he would escape being treated as a common criminal. This meant that he was a comic figure, so ludicrous that only the most gullible would take him for real. Campbell displayed such "comic" black people, in his poem *Ol Doc Hyar:*

> *"Ur ol' Hyar lib in ur house on de hill,*
> *He hunners yurs ol' an' nebber wuz ill;*
> *He yurs dee so long an' he eyes so beeg;*
> *An' he laigs so spry dat he dawnce ur jeeg:*
> *He lib so long dat he know ebbry tings*
> *'Bout de beas'ses dat walks an' de bu'ds dat sings . . ."*

Such a character lacked the ring of truth that the nation needed. It was not enough to laugh at the black man. The face that has been painted upon the clown can never give complete satisfaction. There is always the possibility that the clown may be laughing at you instead of with you. Such was the case with the minstrel man. The slave, however, knew what the master wanted, what he wished to see and wanted to believe and therefore, as James Weldon Johnson wrote, ". . . they provided him with the entertainment fare to suit his fancy: Every plantation had its talented band that could crack jokes and sing and dance to the accompaniment of the banjo and the bones—the bones being the actual ribs of sheep or other small animals cut the proper length, scraped clean and bleached in the sun. When the planter wished to entertain his guests, he needed only to call his troupe of black minstrels."

The same slaves sang other songs, but not for the amusement of the master or his guests. While working under the hot sun in the field or perhaps waiting to "steal away," the minstrel man of the hour before lifted his voice and his heart to his god and performed a war dance instead of a comic ritual. On this stage he displayed more enthusiasm than he had on the master's. Here he poured forth his bitterness and despair—emotions that the clown's mask had hidden. He sang the Negro spirituals, or as Dr. Du Bois called them, the "Sorrow Songs." In the spiritual, the slave gave the lie to the plantation apologists. How can one validate the simplicity of the slave when everywhere he was chanting "steal away to Jesus," those code words which told the runaway that the way was clear to make his move, godspeed, and follow the North Star? How does one argue that the slaves were happy and loyal when such men could be heard out in the field, their voices crackling in the hot summer air singing, "Go Down Moses," and "Didn't My Lord Deliver Daniel?"

These contradictions became apparent to the Southerner after slavery. The South had not been completely fooled into believing its own illusion. Northerners might be enthusiastic about the antics of Mr. Tambo and Mr. Bones—so much so as to make minstrelsy a high-paying profession. They might even accept these clowns in black face—whites who painted their faces black and blacks who painted theirs blacker still for the real thing—but the Southerner needed myths made of stronger stuff. Thus the plantation tradition began.

It had several advantages over the minstrel tradition. Slapstick comedy and buffoonery were underplayed. The black man was still looked upon as a buffoon, but now he was a buffoon whose most important characteristic was his childish simplicity. In transforming him from a clown into a child, the South sought to make their actions more understandable. The child buffoon owed his loyalty not only to the master and his family, but also to the old plantation and the southern way of life. He could no longer be shown as possessing guile in a comic frame—such interpretations had previously concealed his intentions to run away to the North —he now had to be shown as possessing a childlike affection for his superiors and taking a childish approach to all problems.

Here a serious difficulty arose. Although children may need to be held in check and supervised, what is the justification for enslaving them? The necessity for the restriction of liberty under slavery had to be justified. In order to accomplish this end, a character far more vicious than a child was needed. Yet, the system of slavery demanded justification for another argument as well: that it and its successor —segregation—were neither cruel nor vindictive and did not violate the ethics of Christianity. To uphold this belief, a character with the gentleness and loyalty of a child was mandatory.

This was a problem that called for the wisdom of a Solomon; and like Solomon, the South met the problem in a most ingenious way. It was so successful that the entire nation accepted the answer as the final solution: the black man was both child and beast! He was simple-minded, humorous, and childlike from one point of view; while from another, he was a rapist, razor slasher, thief, and murderer.

The South must be given credit for creating a way of maintaining slavery despite its eventual destruction as a system. Think of Cain from Biblical history. Cain is more enslaved than ever when the mark is branded upon his forehead. This mark distinguishes him from his fellow men and relegates him to a special place among them. Even after the act of murder is forgotten, he is still defined as a murderer by the mark on his forehead.

In similar fashion, the South imposed its "mark of Cain" on the black man. It defined him in terms that the nation not only accepted but helped to substantiate by enlisting the aid of its poets and writers. Early in the eighteenth century, John Saffrin of Massachusetts wrote a definition that proved the black man to be an unregenerate criminal:

> *Cowardly and cruel . . .*
> *Prone to revenge, Imp of inveterate hate,*
> *He that exasperates them; soon espies*
> *Mischief and murder in their eyes*
> *Libidinous, Deceitful, False and Rude*
> *The spume issue of ingratitude.*

Saffrin's definition was echoed in the nineteenth century by many, including Thomas Dixon who declared that the black man was "a degenerate, inferior, irresponsible, and bestial creature transformed from a chattel to be bought and sold into a possible beast to be feared and guarded."

Other writers saw the black man as a simple child, a contented darky, and their names read like a Who's Who of American literary folklore: Albion Tourgée, George Washington Cable, Joel Chandler Harris, Harriet Beecher Stowe, Irwin Russell and the song writer, Stephen Foster. The definition becomes meaningful to any one who can recall Foster's depiction of the black man in "My Old Kentucky Home."

However, the definition was not complete. During a period in which the art of oratory was highly regarded, a man's status depended upon his ability to speak well. The Americans, like the English, regarded those whose use of the language was flawless as cultured gentlemen worthy of the title "civilized." What better way to separate the civilized from the uncivilized than to attribute to the latter a quaint, different, amusing, but primitive diction. Negro dialect, a holdover from the minstrel tradition, was given new status and became the foundation of the literature of the plantation tradition.

The tradition was in vogue long before Dunbar began to write. He was fond of saying that he did not create the tradition, and he didn't. Moreover, he never defined black people in the way that Saffrin and Dixon did—none of his black characters are evil or deceitful, none are rapists or murderers. For the most part, they are kind, loving, loyal slaves who look after their masters and their masters' welfare.

Alone in his "garret" in London, destitute and despondent, Dunbar finally realized that one definition was as dangerous and as false as the other. Those beautiful sounding words he had written, "to interpret the soul of my people," had been turned to hollow mockery by his critics. As they saw it, the soul of his people was primitive and perhaps he, its interpreter, was the most primitive of all. What was to be done? So skillful and efficient a dialect poet as he could not cease writing dialect; to do so would mean the loss of his audience as well as his chance for fame and fortune. It is difficult to say how long he wrestled with this problem but, once he arrived at the unmistakable conclusion that his freedom was being encroached upon, he resorted to quiet, private rebellion.

The rebellion, however, had to be carried out subtly, with the craftiness he attributed to some of his characters. What better way to make a plea for freedom from dialect than to produce a work in which dialect was missing altogether? What better way to rebel against the restrictions placed upon him by his critics than to create, in fiction, a situation in which someone like himself is restricted by tyranny? But most ironic of all, why not make his characters white, creating a situation in which a black man pleads for a white man's freedom?

Among the many requests for his work, was one from Lippincott asking for a novel to be published in serial form. Very well, he would write the novel. The germ of such a project had been floating around in his mind for some time. Now the thoughts began to crystallize. He would call his novel *The Uncalled*, and although the characters would be white, the experiences would be his. Would the critics understand the deeper meaning behind this title? Perhaps not. Yet, he would strike a blow for freedom, and in doing so silence, for a while at least, the quiet desperation in his own heart.

He worked on the novel whenever he was free from the constant task of finding a way to get back to America other than by swimming. He had other commitments for poems, articles, and stories, and he worked on these also. One day, while strolling through the British Museum, he met two other black Americans, Dr. Alexander Crummell and Hallie Q. Brown. They were members of a group that had come from Washington for the Jubilee Celebration. Crummell was to remain in England for several months, and as soon as the poet told him of his difficulties, he invited Dunbar to move into the house he had rented. Thus, the pressing problem of room and board was at least temporarily solved.

Thanks to Dr. Crummell, he was not only financially free, but somewhat mentally free as well. After long hours of writing, he relaxed by visiting England's tourist attractions. He went first to Westminster Abbey where many English poets are enshrined. He went to Buckingham Palace to watch the famous changing of the guards. He went to the Cheshire Cheese, the tavern where in times past the English critic Samuel Johnson often came to eat, drink, and debate. While walking through the English countryside and again while at Westminster Abbey, he had felt a boyish delight at the realization that he stood on the hallowed ground of some of the world's most famous poets.

His romantic young mind took him back through the years and enabled him to form a relationship with the English masters of sentiment and the spoken word. This was the native land of those who had been his first inspiration, whose verse had first alerted him to the world of nature. This was the land of Shelley, Pope, Tennyson, Byron, Browning, and Keats. Of these poets he most admired John Keats, the young doctor turned poet, whose poems, melodic and haunting, were filled with images of love, pain, and despair. Perhaps, he also recalled that Keats had lived a life of quiet desperation, that he suffered from tuberculosis, warred against vindictive critics, and having been defeated in love and ambition, out of sense of total and complete despair, resigned himself to oblivion. "My name," he had written, "has been writ on water." The world neither praised Keats during his lifetime, nor granted him recognition for the things that he attempted. How similar and yet dissimilar was Keats' life to his own? The world had already recognized Dunbar, and was now praising him; yet, it had done so for all the wrong reasons.

As he reflected on the lives of the poets and their verse, as he traveled the countryside observing in its free state, nature, it was natural that his thoughts should turn to Alice. And when thinking of Alice and the English poets, it was also natural that he should think of Robert and Elizabeth Barrett Browning. Browning had dared all for his Elizabeth, an invalid girl whose poems had caught the young poet's eye. Once in love with her, nothing could prevent his having her for his own, not even a protesting father. One night he took her away—stole her away would be more accurate. Destiny was kind; the two lived, loved, and sang together.

And he and his Alice? What did destiny have in store for them? "Sunshine or shadow, or gold day or gray day/Life must be lived as our destinies rule," he had written. Did he believe this any longer? Could not a destiny that sought to rob him of that which he loved be altered? Wasn't that what was meant by *Invictus*, a poem he praised above all others? Henley had written, "I am the master of my fate;/I am the captain of my soul." Didn't this hold true in love, if nowhere else? Wasn't long life, health, and love due him and Alice as compensation for their devotion to one another, for their faith in one another, even as many private wars erupted around them?

He thought of her often now. He wished that she were there. How happy they would be together in the fields of daisies and dandelions where birds offered their song morning, noon, and night. "Love hath the wings of a butterfly" he had written at a time when, as now, his heart had been filled with the things of love. Like the butterfly who longs to light upon its favorite flower, Dunbar longed for the moment when he would leave England behind, return to Alice, pluck her from among all the other flowers, and make her his forever.

He left England in June of 1897, five months after his arrival. He was still young—twenty-four years old and still very much in love.

V

I KNOW WHAT THE CAGED BIRD FEELS

*I know why the caged bird beats his wing
Till its blood is red on the cruel bars;
For he must fly back to his perch and cling
When he fain would be on the bow a-swing.*

Dunbar returned from England to find that his popularity had increased greatly. Not only were there numerous requests for poems and short stories, there was also an equal number of requests for articles about his trip to England. Many magazines wanted him to compare racial conditions in England with those in America. He obliged and wrote a few articles such as "England as Seen by a Black Man," which was published in September of 1897.

He had been back from England only a short time before Will Cook—with whom he had worked some two years before in setting "A Negro Love Song" to music—and his brother sought him out. They found him in Washington at the home of Professor Kelly Miller of Howard University. They implored him to resume work on their musical *Clorindy*. He agreed, and the three men began work under the inquisitive eyes of the Miller household. After the musical was completed, Will and John Cook rushed back to New York to begin casting and holding auditions. The show opened at the Casino Roof Garden in New York in the summer of 1898.

Two days prior to the completion of *Clorindy*, Dunbar received a letter from Colonel Robert G. Ingersoll. A lawyer who had once been a dispenser of patronage for the

Republican party, Ingersoll had received a copy of *Oak and Ivy* from Tobey. He inquired into the history of the author and, struck by the fact that so talented a young man worked as an elevator operator, set about to secure him more favorable and distinguished employment. His efforts were successful, and on October 1, 1897, Dunbar began work as an assistant in the reading room of the Library of Congress. His salary was seven hundred and twenty dollars a year. The last obstacle which stood between him and Alice had now been removed.

Because of his financial state, Dunbar had hesitated to get married. Although he enjoyed immense popularity and had a wide reading audience, he was not yet able to earn a living by his pen alone. *Lyrics of Lowly Life* was well received. *The Uncalled* was finished and sent to Lippincott's. There was a collection of short stories, *Folks from Dixie*, ready to follow *The Uncalled* to press. In terms of financial rewards, however, there was little; and what there was went to pay debts and to purchase a new home in Washington for his mother and his bride-to-be.

His debts were many, and there was no one to whom he owed more than Tobey. What he owed Tobey could not be counted in money alone. Tobey had sent him the money that enabled him to leave England. When he had finally made contact with Miss Pond, who was by then in Paris, she repeated her suggestion that he swim the Atlantic Ocean. She accused him of breaking his contract with her by appearing under the sponsorship of others than herself. She did not recall that she had left him stranded while she went off to Paris, or that he had been forced to take what few readings he could get from anyone who would secure them for him. She insisted that she was not obligated to supply him with a return ticket, and with that final word, she sailed back to America alone.

Once again finding himself "in desperate straits," he had cabled Tobey. As he had done so many times in the past, Tobey responded quickly and positively. He wired the forsaken poet enough money to return home, and when Dunbar reached America Tobey lent him enough more to tide him over until he began to realize a profit from his works. The first of his writings to produce a substantial amount of money was *Lyrics of Lowly Life*. The initial returns were small, yet more than he had ever received previously. Over the years his earnings from *Lyrics of Lowly Life* mounted, for the book sold ten thousand copies per year for about five years. However, the book was important in a much more meaningful way: it brought him national fame and a national audience.

That a great deal of this acclaim was due to William Dean Howells is a point beyond dispute. *Lyrics of Lowly Life* was, as Benjamin Brawley observed, "a beautiful little volume . . . attractive in form and having a regular imprint. . . ." The content, however, differed little in substantial ways from the previous two volumes. In terms of form, the book was a mixture of poems in standard English and dialect. The difference between this arrangement and that of the previous books—and it was probably due to the ingenuity of the editors—was that the dialect pieces were not separated into special sections. The oak and the ivy were intertwined, the majors and the minors were one. There were one hundred and five poems, ninety-four of which had previously appeared in *Oak and Ivy* and *Majors and Minors*.

There were two major distinctions between this book and

its predecessors; first, the book was published by Dodd, Mead & Company, a major publishing house. Second, the introduction was written by William Dean Howells. After Dodd, Mead had been persuaded to publish *Lyrics of Lowly Life,* Major Pond, shrewd promoter that he was, had asked Howells to write the introduction. Howells agreed. He was so certain that the remarks he had made about *Majors and Minors* would hold true for all of Dunbar's works, that he composed an introduction without first reading the book! The introduction was a rewrite of the previous article, differing only in minor details.

As he had done in the first article, Howells began the second by minimizing the appeal of the book by reason of the author's race, religion, or color. "The world is too old" he stated, ". . . to care for the work of a poet because he is black." Yet, in spite of this statement, Howells goes on to make a special appeal based on racial grounds alone: "So far as I could remember," he continued, "Paul Dunbar was the only man of pure African blood and of American civilization to feel the Negro life aesthetically and express it lyrically."

Not only is this statement untrue, but throughout the years it has done incalculable damage in the field of education. Because of it Afro-American children have been led to believe that black literature—and especially black poetry —began with Paul Laurence Dunbar. Dunbar has been hailed in the public schools, black and white, as the only real black poet in America before Langston Hughes and the poets of the Harlem Renaissance. Some people have gone so far as to claim that he was the only successful black writer until the twentieth century.

The facts are completely different. In 1881 Frederick Douglass published his autobiography, *The Life and Times of Frederick Douglass,* in lyrical, flowing prose. William

Wells Brown wrote the novel *Clotel* in 1853; Martin Delany, *Blake or the Huts of America* in 1859. Francis Ellen Watkins Harper, Dunbar's contemporary and, like him, a poet and novelist, wrote *Iola Leroy* in 1892. Another contemporary of Dunbar's was Charles W. Chesnutt, who was contributing short stories to the *Atlantic Monthly* at the same time that Howells was making false claims about Dunbar.

The fact that Dunbar and Chesnutt were contemporaries must be emphasized. They both wrote during the same period, yet Dunbar's name is a household word, while Chesnutt's is known to very few. This state of affairs cannot be explained away by the argument that one was a poet and the other primarily a writer of fiction. (Dunbar wrote as much fiction as Chesnutt, although his reputation rests mainly on his poetry.) What is far more important is that both wrote in the plantation tradition. However, in Chesnutt's works, the black characters are not comic darkies but more closely approach the "realistic portrayal" of black people that Howells claimed for Dunbar.

Chesnutt's *The Conjure Woman* is a good example. The book contains seven stories, all narrated by Uncle Julius, in the fashion of Uncle Remus, the character created by Joel Chandler Harris. If we are familiar with Uncle Remus, then we are familiar with Aunt Joshy, Mammy Peggy, and Uncle Simon—characters from Dunbar's two collections of short stories, *Folks from Dixie* and *The Strength of Gideon*. However, Chesnutt uses Uncle Julius to correct the false impression caused by Uncle Remus. Uncle Julius is a wily old ex-slave. He does not tell tales for the entertainment of his employers, a prosperous white couple, but instead designs his tales to bring some special benefit to himself or, in one case, to a favored nephew. Like the animal stories the slaves used to tell each other, the story indicates how the black man has tried to outwit the white.

Chesnutt was only one of the prose writers who either preceded Dunbar or were his contemporaries. There were also poets. There were the collective poets, those unknown men, women, and children who composed the spirituals —works of poetry unsurpassed in American literature— which tell, as Du Bois has written, "of death and suffering and unvoiced longing toward a truer world, of misty wanderings and hidden ways." There were individual poets. Lucy Terry, a young slave girl, was the first, but Phillis Wheatley who was about seven years old when purchased, is perhaps the best known. One year after having been brought to America from Senegal, she had learned enough English to enable her to read the Bible. Two years later at the age of eleven, she wrote her first poem.

There was also Jupiter Hammon, a slave who lived in Queens Village, New York, whose poetry preceded that of Phillis Wheatley. Yet, of the two, she was the better poet. In fact, her poetry proves that she was a better poet than many of her white contemporaries—in particular Philip Freneau and Anne Bradstreet who are often praised by the Howellses of the world for their poetical talents. There was George Moses Horton, the first "angry black poet" in America, who questioned the universe that doomed him to slavery in such bitter lines as the following: "Alas! And am I born for this/ To wear this slavish chain!" Also a poet of humor, as *My Little Duck Boots* shows, he foreshadowed Dunbar as a singer of sensuous love lyrics.

Francis E. W. Harper, novelist and poet, although not the technician that Dunbar was, wrote poetry which, if these lines from her poem *Bury Me in a Free Land* are indicative, was more truthful and relevant to black people.

I ask no monument, proud and high
To arrest the gaze of the passerby
All that my yearning spirit craves
Is bury me not in a land of slaves.

Howells had singled out Dunbar's dialect poetry for special praise; but even in this area there were black men who wrote dialect poetry before Dunbar. One of them, James Campbell, reproduced the speech of the plantation slaves much better than Dunbar. One stanza from Campbell's *Negro Serenade* illustrates this point.

O, honey lub, my turkel dub,
  Doan' you hyuh my bownjer ringin',
While de night-dew falls an' de ho'n owl calls
  By de ol' ba'n gate Ise singin'.

With the exception of Phillis Wheatley, none of these poets possessed technical skill equal to that of Dunbar; yet each portrayed aspects of black life as accurately—even more accurately—than he, and Campbell, Mrs. Harper, and Horton did so more truthfully.

Howells' damning with faint praise did not annoy Dunbar. What did bother him was Howells' commentary on his poetry in which he praised the dialect pieces above those in standard English.

This is the one element of Howells' criticism that stands out in both articles. In each, he approached this section of the essay in the same manner. He began with the poems written in standard English. Except for "the race of the author," he explained, they were not very distinguishable from the "pieces of most young poets." After quoting a few lines from *Conscience and Remorse,* Howells hurried on to applaud the poems written in dialect.

"Yet it appeared to me then, and it appears to me now, that there is a precious difference of temperament between the races which it would be a great pity ever to lose, and that this is best preserved and most charmingly suggested by Mr. Dunbar in those pieces of his where he studies the moods and traits of his race in its own accent of our English." Howells, having thus laid the racial foundation, proceeds to tell the audience what he means by dialect: ". . . delightful personal attempts and failure for the written and spoken language." Moreover, Howells equates the souls of black people with dialect language: "In nothing is his essentially refined and delicate art so well shown as in these pieces, which as I ventured to say, described the range between appetite and emotion . . . which is the range of the race. He reveals in these a finely ironical perception of the Negro's limitations." He concludes the introduction to *Lyrics of Lowly Life* by intermingling praise and insult: "These [dialect pieces] are divinations and reports of what passes in the hearts and minds of a lowly people . . . I cannot undertake to prophesy [Mr. Dunbar's future performance] but if he should do nothing more than he has done, I should feel that he had made the strongest claim for the Negro in English literature that the Negro has yet made."

On July 4th, seven days after the introduction had been written, Dunbar attended a party given in his honor by Dr. Tobey. There were over sixty guests present, among them, Mayor Jones, Brand Whitlock, and the Governor of Ohio. Dr. Tobey knew that the young poet stood on the threshold of fame, and that he was anxious and somewhat frightened. He wanted to buoy Dunbar's spirits. He had seen many men who, caught up in the whirlwind of sudden fame, had snapped under the pressure. His sanitorium was filled with such men. He took Dunbar aside and, during the brief chat related his fears. Dunbar assured Tobey that he was all right, that all he needed was a little sleep. Tobey, satisfied by the response, left the poet to make his way to bed.

He did not sleep, however. He sat down and wrote a poem, which he titled *The Crisis*. It was as if he sensed a crisis in his life at this point. The last stanza reads:

> *"Mere human strength may stand ill-fortune's frown;*
> *So I prevailed, for human strength was mine;*
> *But from the killing pow'r of great renown,*
> *Naught may protect me save a strength divine.*
> *Help me, O Lord, in this my trembling cause;*
> *I scorn men's curses, but I dread applause!"*

Benjamin Brawley believes that the poem was written "with the humility of one conscious of a great blessing." The poem *was* written with humility, of that there is little doubt. Whether or not it was written by "one conscious of a great blessing" is indeed doubtful. Fame was being bought at too dear a price—he was being praised for all the wrong reasons. Moreover, the praise was not only insulting to him; it was also insulting to his people. The introduction, which had begun by minimizing race, had made race the most important element. Dunbar had been praised for interpreting the soul of his people when, perhaps, few black people knew as little about the souls of their people as he did.

With the exception of the Chicago World's Fair, Dunbar at that time had never been further than six hundred miles outside of Dayton. Never had he traveled south, never had he seen a plantation or a cotton field. All of his high school classmates had been white; and now, as then, with the ex-

ception of Dr. Robert (Bud) Burns, most of his friends were
white. What little he knew of the good old days of the
antebellum South, of the characters who peopled his stories
was gleaned from accounts related to him by his mother
and father. He had distorted these to gain his hearing.

And what of dialect? The true language of his people?
He had never heard dialect spoken; at least not the kind
that he used in his poetry and short stories. His mother had
been a slave, but she did not speak in dialect; neither did
his father. None of the black men whom he admired—
Frederick Douglass, Alexander Crummell, Booker T. Washington—spoke dialect. He did not even speak it himself. And
so a crisis of a different sort loomed large in his life. He
stepped up to the door of fame and halted, deliberated. Like
a soft white downy blanket, the world of success lay waiting
to embrace him. A nameless, faceless audience was out there
waiting to hear him, to listen to his songs. If only they
waited to hear his songs of love, of joy, of despair. How he
could write these with happiness, with carefree abandon.
He would labor over them as hard as his mother had labored
over the neighbors' laundry. These were the poems he admired—if only that unseen audience would listen to them.

They would not, and he knew it. Most of them believed
that black people were ignorant and uncultured, and they
wanted him to verify this fact for them. They would listen
to his songs in dialect, read his stories about folks from Dixie
because, in them, they could find evidence to substantiate
their own widely held beliefs. He began to realize that this
world would rather listen to and praise "a jingle in a broken
tongue" than words "with now and then, a deeper note."

He would have to satisfy them. Whatever his misgivings
or hostilities, he had no choice but to write what they

wanted to read. He had little education, no money, and no family connections. He had a mother, grown old and tired through poverty and hard work; there was a young woman whom he wished to marry whose parents did not want her to marry him because he had neither wealth nor position. Before him was the dubious possibility of fame, which would have to be bought at a terrible price—the surrender of his poetical soul. Behind him were his past experiences in which prospects had been dim indeed—the opportunity for an elevator job or one similar to it in which the only reward was to grow old, bitter, and cynical about what might have been.

He made the only choice that he could. He would entertain his audience. He would titillate their fancies and ease their consciences. He would tell them what they wanted to hear. However, when they were least aware, he would write other things, pose serious questions:

> ". . . *of life, serenely sweet,*
> *With, now and then, a deeper note*
> *From some high peak, nigh yet remote*
> [*and voice*] *the world's absorbing beat.*"

He eventually wrote William Dean Howells and thanked the critic for writing the introduction for him. The letter was short, less than four paragraphs. He acknowledged his indebtedness for the critic's help and told him of his plans for the future. In general his tone was courteous and respectful, but two lines, which more nearly reflect the crisis of conscience that Dunbar was having at the time, stand out from the others: "The kindly praise that you have accorded me will be an incentive to more careful work. My greatest fear is that you may have been more kind to me than just." There is, as the poet well knew, a sharp dividing line between justice and kindness.

Thanks to Howells' introduction, *Lyrics of Lowly Life* was well received. The book opens with a poem in standard English, *Ere Sleep Comes Down to Soothe the Weary Eyes,* and closes with the dialect poem from which Howells had quoted at length, *The Party.* Perhaps the most important poem in the volume is *Unexpressed.* It had previously appeared in *Majors and Minors* and received little notice by the critics. Yet, it is fundamental to an analysis of the crisis that Dunbar was undergoing. The poem is short, consisting of only three stanzas.

Deep in my heart that aches with the repression,
And strives with plenitude of bitter pain,
There lives a thought that clamors for expression,
And spends its undelivered force in vain.

What boots it that some other may have thought it?
The right of thoughts expression is divine;
The price of pain I pay for it has bought it,
I care not who lays claim to it—'t is mine!

And yet not mine until it be delivered;
The manner of its birth shall prove the test,
Alas, alas, my rock of pride is shivered—
I beat my brow—the thought still unexpressed.

The thought of love had been expressed, however! In letter after letter to his fiancée, Dunbar restated his love for her, imploring her to agree to marriage. Alice, who was then teaching school in Brooklyn, New York, was sincerely dedicated to her work. Over sixty youngsters were in her classes and her heart belonged to each of them. They were all less fortunate than she had been as a child. Few had parents who were preparing them for what lay ahead or guiding them along the right road in a hostile society. She had been armored against the world, given the resources with which to protect herself. Yet, even she had felt the rocks that the world hurled unceasingly at those with black skins. If the world had gotten to her despite her armor, what would happen to her pupils who had none?

The future did not appear very hopeful! Strange sounds concerning the education of black children were being heard across the country. Booker T. Washington, the most powerful and influential black man in America, had declared that black children should be taught to work with their hands. The nation interpreted this to mean that blacks should be educated to become domestic workers, factory workers, and handymen; to perform the low kinds of menial labor that white people did not want to perform. In this, the nation went further than Washington. He had not argued explicitly that black people were incapable of mastering the professions. He had only implied that their best opportunity for security in a racist society lay in becoming efficient in those jobs that whites did not want to undertake.

The nation believed differently. Black men should be servants because they were incapable of being anything more. They could not lead themselves, could not learn the fine art of running governments, could not compete on an equal footing with whites in the business world, and could not achieve prominence in the world of science and letters. Better then to send black children to schools that taught handicrafts and mechanics, sewing and housekeeping, than to waste their time in institutions of higher learning. This the nation believed; and this the nation had the power to make a reality.

Alice had little doubt on this score. The country maintained that there was a place for blacks in the society. It defined that place and made every effort to see that blacks were educated only for that specific place. She thought about her fiance and what this had meant for him. Unless blacks are quite lucky, the places designed for them by the American society were not behind desks, at ticket windows, or in the offices of large corporations. They were on elevator stools, in kitchens, or in offices where a broom was a necessary part of the workers' uniform. Blacks were not expected to demand anything else. If, like Dunbar, they were unfortunate enough to have been educated for other employment, they were losers. There was nothing else to be had. Their education was of little use unless it fitted them for menial jobs.

The trap was closed tightly about Alice's students and there was little she could do about it. She did as much as she could. She treated each child as though he were special, as if he were her own. She tried to give him encouragement and strength, to brace him for what she knew lay ahead. This was all she could do, for she was caught in the trap with them, no matter how much the world denied it. Therefore, she was not receptive to the pressures her fiance's letters subjected her to daily. They had decided at the time of the engagement to be married in June. Alice thought that this was a good plan. It would give her time to persuade her parents that her love for him was so strong that she was determined to marry him despite their opposition. It would also afford her time to complete the school year and to finish the job she was attempting to do, almost singlehandedly, with her students.

Dunbar's letters became more insistent. He had begun his new job at the Library of Congress and, according to biographer Jean Gould, ". . . the flowers of fame began to be heaped upon Paul Dunbar. He was asked to speak before organizations as well as to give readings. Magazines and newspapers carried articles about him, and by him. The Washington *Post* printed a full column, which called him the 'Orpheus of His Race' . . . Magazines asked for short stories and serials, publishing houses for novels. He called these years his 'pouring time' because so many opportunities poured in on him from all sides."

The "pouring time" began in 1898. The rewards were such as to convince the poet that the money from his writing in addition to his yearly salary, was sufficient to enable him to support his mother and bride-to-be in reasonable comfort. He bought a house in Washington and later sent to Dayton for his mother. He increased the number of his letters to Alice. She was caught between his insistence on the one hand and the recalcitrance of her parents on the other. Her students were in the middle. How could she satisfy one without hurting the others? She desired to please them all. She wanted to marry Dunbar, to reconcile herself and her parents, and to finish the work she had begun with her students.

She set about to devise a plan which would accomplish all her objectives. She would secretly marry in March, return to finish the semester with her students, and in June she would inform her parents that she and Dunbar had been married all along, thus leaving them with little option other than to approve her actions. After deciding upon this course of action she sent the poet a one-word telegram. Boldly, dramatically, in large type, the word was: "Come!"

For Dunbar, the one word was more than enough. The years of indecision were almost at an end. The picture that had attracted him years ago had, like Cinderella, turned into a beautiful princess. As he boarded the train for New York, he was happier than at anytime since the publication of *Lyrics of Lowly Life.*

He and Alice were married on March 6, in a service at the home of the Bishop of the African Methodist Church, W. B. Derrick. Only the minister, his wife, and the bride and groom were present. At the ceremony's end, he sealed their marriage with the same ring he had used to seal their engagement. The gold ring, belonging to his mother, had served at two of the most important events of his life. "With this ring, I thee wed!" he repeated after the bishop, ending the secret ceremony and beginning a new life for himself with another person.

At that moment there was little reminder of the storm that had preceded the marriage; yet the scars of the battle that had been waged between Alice and her parents were deep ones, which would not heal soon. Her parents were not happy that their daughter was to wed a poet—especially one who had had such humble beginnings. Publishers and critics throughout the country made much of Dunbar's previous employment. In describing him, the phrase "one-time elevator boy" was used synonymously with the phrase, "Negro poet." In addition, there was the question of his education. He had finished high school—a great accomplishment for a child of a poor family, black or white, in the nineteenth century. Alice, however, was a college graduate. Added to these difficulties, as Alice's parents saw it, were others. In America, poets were not held in high esteem. They were appreciated by the sophisticated, the college-educated, but rarely by people from the general walk of life. To the average American, poets were queer creatures unlike average folks, to be shunned if not ignored altogether.

Nor were Alice's parents alone in their opposition to the union. Dunbar's mother, Matilda, was not as sold on the idea of the marriage as some of the poet's biographers would have us believe. Although she would never stand in the way of her son's happiness, she nevertheless harbored vague doubts at times as to the wisdom of a marriage between a college woman and her son. She still remembered the divisions that had been caused by slavery. The slave masters had set up divisions among black people, placing those whom they called "house niggers" on one side, and "field niggers" on the other. The "house niggers" were the aristocrats of the plantation system; they worked in the master's house and shared more fully in the plantation life than did the "field niggers," who worked long hours in the field and suffered from the sun and the overseer's lash.

Matilda had been a house Negro. While other black children worked in the fields beside their parents, Matilda sat at the feet of Squire Glass along with his white children, listening to him read stories of knights and ladies. The line was different now; a new aristocracy had been born. The "field niggers" were the poor—those who worked with their hands, and those who had little education. Those who had money, government jobs, and education were the house Negroes. What, then, would Alice, educated and coming from a respectable home, think of her, Matilda, a washerwoman deserted by her husband and forced to quit night school in order to feed and clothe her children? Was she not certain to be "biggity?" Would she not try to lord it over both the Dunbars? Matilda had been apprehensive about the coming marriage, and had sometimes wished that the ceremony would never take place.

The honeymoon was short. Dunbar went back to Washington, Alice to her teaching post in Brooklyn. Yet, in time she became disturbed about her plan. It was successful, and this was what bothered her. She realized that the plan was devious and dishonest, and she recoiled from the fact that she was deceiving her parents. She wrote them a letter in which she explained everything; she told them what she had done and why. She begged them to understand and to forgive her; yet she intimated that the deed was done and that she had no regrets.

She had acted in an ill manner towards her students also. She had wanted to divide her affection between them and her husband. However, she discovered that it was impossible to live in a divided house. If she continued to do what had to be done for them while part of her heart was many miles away in Washington, she and they would suffer. Because she could no longer give them her full attention, she resigned from her job. She hoped that they would find an abler champion than herself. Without hesitation she wired Dunbar to prepare to meet her at the Washington railroad station. He needed no notice; there was no preparation to be made. He was overjoyed at her decision. And finally, in a letter to his long-time friend, Tobey, dated April 6, 1898, Dunbar rejoiced: "All had come around all right now and my wife will be with me on the eighteenth. My announcement cards will go out then. Mother is quite enthusiastic, and my mother-in-law has yielded and gracefully accepted the situation."

VI

THE ORPHEUS OF THE RACE

> *We sit at Life's boards with our*
> *nerves highstrung,*
> *And we play for the stake of fame.*

"But I don't feel famous," Dunbar remarked to his wife. They had completed a whirlwind tour of recitals, readings, and personal appearances. He was famous, of this there could be little doubt. He was only twenty-seven, yet the nation had opened up her heart and ears to him and applauded him as she has never applauded a black poet either before or since. Everywhere he went he was met with acclaim. He was awarded an honorary degree by Atlanta University. He was a guest speaker at a banquet in honor of a congressman from North Carolina. He was invited to participate in several conferences dealing with the education of the Negro. He gave readings of his poetry in New York, Alabama, Kentucky, Ohio, and Massachusetts.

In the summer of 1898, *Clorindy*, the musical which he had worked on with Will and John Cook, opened at the Casino Roof Garden in New York. Dunbar and his wife were present on opening night. They sat in the special box seats reserved for authors and their guests. As Dunbar listened to the lyrics that he had helped to write, he felt a sense of embarrassment. The musical was in the worst of the minstrel tradition. Not only were black people laughing at themselves, they were also performing on stage, offering themselves as objects for the laughter of others. The tunes for which he had written the lyrics were not much more offensive than some of his dialect poems—although, in these he had avoided making his people into buffoons. Still there was a great deal of difference between writing a poem and reciting it, and watching the same poem acted out on a stage. The all-black cast, including the great Afro-American star Ernest Hogan, was very talented and performed well. However, the musical was not a serious work. The titles of the songs illustrate this fact: "The Hottest Coon in Dixie," "Love in a Cottage Is Best," "Who Dat Say Chicken in a Crowd." In addition, among his contributions was "A Negro Love Song," which he had written in a humorous vein. Listening to it now, in this setting, it sounded not humorous, but ridiculous. *Clorindy* caused Dunbar to doubt the claim to fame which others made for him. In his own eyes he had not achieved success and never would.

Yet *Clorindy* was highly successful. It ran on Broadway throughout the summer, and played to capacity audiences. The songs from the musical became hits overnight. People hummed them, memorized lines from them, and the "Cakewalk," a dance featured in the musical, became famous throughout America. Songs from the musical were adopted by other musicians, and the famous dancing team of Williams and Walker added their names to the list of important black entertainers who used the score from *Clorindy* in their acts.

Dunbar despaired over his contribution to the musical, and he vowed that he would never write lyrics for another such show. Harry Burleigh, the Negro composer and a friend of the poet's, had told him once that minstrel tunes were a menace to true Negro music. Dunbar knew that such lyrics were a threat to black poetry. He would have no more of them. *Clorindy* would be his last "coon show."

There were other disappointments besides *Clorindy*,

some of a much more serious nature. The country welcomed him as a singer of songs, as the Orpheus of his race; yet, it also regarded him as a Negro, one who was still subject to the indignities that his people were daily forced to undergo. Even though his name was Paul Laurence Dunbar, he was still expected to ride Jim Crow cars, to eat in segregated restaurants, and to room in segregated hotels. This was as true in the North as it was in the South.

On one such occasion he had been invited by Mrs. Merrill, a local patron of the arts in Albany, New York, to give a reading. When he arrived in Albany on the day scheduled for the recital, he asked a black bus driver to let him off at the Kenmore hotel. The bus driver, a native of the city, was familiar with the town's customs. Repeatedly, he questioned the poet as to the nature of his business at the Kenmore. Dunbar's answers were so conclusive that the driver finally shook his head and attended to his driving. He thought that his passenger was either lying or insane.

Once at the hotel, Dunbar became aware of the reasons for the driver's insistent questions. When he walked in and put his bag down, the clerk glared at him suspiciously. He picked up the pen to register and the man bellowed out in a hostile tone of voice: "Hold on! What are you going to do?" Dunbar remained calm. "To register, of course," he replied. "You can't register here," said the clerk. "We have no rooms for you in this hotel."

However, rooms had been reserved in the name of Paul Laurence Dunbar. Having verified this astonishing fact, the clerk's rage became greater, and he scowled at the poet, gestured obscenely, and finally summoned the manager. The manager was equally outraged. Looking Dunbar up and down, the manager said, "This Negro is crazy. Telephone to the police station and let them come up and get him." Before this action could be taken, Mrs. Merrill appeared and put an end to the confusion. She demanded that her guest be accorded the same courtesy granted to any other guest.

The victory was satisfying; yet the wounds would never heal. Fame was not a stepping stone to dignity—not for a black man. This thought was now brought home to him frequently. The world would buy his wares, but it would look with scorn upon the bearer of those wares for no other reason than that his skin was black.

During these times, he thought of his recent trip to England. He wished that he could have made a living there so that he could have sent for his mother and wife, and the three of them might have lived free from bigotry and discrimination. It was too late for that now. This burden he would bear along with the others. All that he could do was to search for some way to lighten his load. He had once believed that he could speak to the country through another voice—from behind a white face. In his novel, *The Uncalled*, the major character was named Freddie Brent, but except for the fact that he was white, the character might as well have been called Paul Laurence Dunbar.

That novel was among his favorites, and he wanted his audience to regard it as highly as he did. More than any of the others, it was a plea for sympathy, for understanding. Initially, it appeared in serial form in *Lippincott's Magazine*. The last installment was completed and published in May 1898. Dodd, Mead & Company released the story in book form later in the same year. Much later in 1898 came *Folks from Dixie*, a collection of short stories. Many of the stories, relying heavily on dialect and stereotypic characters, had previously appeared in *Cosmopolitan* magazine, among others. The reviews of *The Uncalled* were mostly unfavorable; those of *Folks from Dixie*, hailed the stories as "great works of art."

Begun in England, *The Uncalled* was finished in America. The hero of the story is a young orphan, Freddie Brent, and the story is set in a "small town" called Dexter, Ohio. Frederick, the son of Tom and Margaret Brent, is orphaned at the age of five. Before the novel begins, we are informed by the author that Margaret had run away from her husband for Tom was an alcoholic and given to frequent brawling. After his wife leaves him, Tom also leaves the town of Dexter. Shortly after his departure, Margaret dies. Friends and neighbors gather to decide the fate of young Freddie. They decide to make the child the ward of the town spinster, Hester Prime, a deeply religious, strict, and demanding woman.

She raises Freddie in the ways of the church and demands strict obedience to church gospel as well as to her own rules at home, modeled after those of the church. She is aided in caring for the boy by a one-time sweetheart, Eliphalet Hodges, whom she finally consents to marry. Hodges is the opposite of Hester. He encourages Freddie to obey his instincts, to always make his own decisions. Freddie's past—and especially the bad character of his father—hangs like a curse over his head. The townspeople will never allow him to forget that his father was a drunkard —a sinner who transgressed the laws of Dexter and God. Neither will Hester. They continue to prophesy that Freddie, like his father, will turn out bad.

They are disappointed. Freddie is sent to a religious school against his will—Hester's decision—but excels in his class nevertheless. He is such a good student that he is offered the pastorship of Dexter Baptist Church, upon the retirement of the Reverend Mr. Simpson. Mr. Simpson is also the father of Freddie's fiancée, Elizabeth. This is the high point of the story. Freddie's triumph is doubly sweet. Hester, who never had children of her own, had taken the son of a sinner and made him into a man of God—proving the gossips and prophets wrong. Not only did Freddie escape his father's destiny, but he even turned out better than the other boys of Dexter, who had no albatrosses about their necks. However, this high point marks the beginning of Freddie's downfall.

He has never wanted to become a minister. He does so against his will due to the old spinster's prodding and then finds that he cannot live up to the strict Calvinist rules of the church. When he is called upon by influential members of the church, including the former minister, his prospective father-in-law, to denounce from the pulpit a woman who gave birth to an illegitimate child, he refuses. After a hearing before a committee of the church, he resigns the office of minister. Because Elizabeth sided with her father and the townspeople, he breaks their engagement. Finally, he leaves Dexter and ends up in Cincinnati.

In Cincinnati he obtains a room at a boarding house. A fellow boarder suggests that they take a walk around the town. During the tour Freddie is handed a leaflet inviting the public to attend a meeting being held by the members of the temperance society. Freddie leaves his friend and goes to the meeting. The meeting is an old-fashioned revival in which various individuals who have fallen into sin come forward to confess, after which the crowd breaks into praying and singing. One of the speakers is the man who had given Freddie the invitation. The man calls himself the "California Pilgrim." Yet, he begins to talk about his life in a city called Dexter, Ohio—his sinful ways, his drinking and brawling, and his desertion of his wife and child. In conclusion, the old man announces that he plans to go back to Dexter to seek forgiveness.

Freddie is shocked. He realizes that the "California Pilgrim" is his father. In addition, this man is now about to return to Dexter to add further disgrace to the Brent name. A few days later, still not having recovered from the shocking experience, he receives a telegram from Dexter. His father has taken a room with the Hodges and is close to death. Freddie is requested to come at once. He goes home, still filled with bitterness at the memory of his father's actions. But, when he sees his father—gazes upon that sick, emaciated form—he is overcome with remorse. He forgives his father on his death bed. Freddie leaves Dexter a second time. In a letter to Hester and Eliphalet he tells them of his good fortune after leaving his hometown. He is soon to be married to a wonderful girl named Alice, and he has joined a Congregational church. At the end of the novel, Eliphalet arrives for the wedding service and embraces the young couple.

Lida Keck Wiggins, Dunbar's earliest biographer, was the first to point out the similarities between the life of Frederick Brent and that of Paul Laurence Dunbar. According to Mrs. Wiggins, both were being pushed into a profession for which they felt uncalled. Like Hester Prime, Matilda Dunbar had wanted her son to be a minister. Barring this, she wanted him to become a doctor. Dunbar had entertained notions of becoming a lawyer. In the nineteenth century, these were among the few professions to which black men might aspire. Teaching was another. In each instance, such professionals would work with and among their own people. This meant that their contact with whites would be minimal. The sons of less-affluent black people usually chose the ministry. To be a minister did not require that a man be educated, but only that he be "called."

That Matilda Dunbar wanted her son to be a minister is not surprising. An ex-slave, she looked upon the minister as the important man he had been during slavery. On many plantations the black minister was the only one available, and he preached to white and black alike. On each plantation, he was the exhorter who warned his congregation of the consequences of evil doing, of what would befall those who sinned, and of the glories available in the world to come.

Frequently, he was the instrument of the master. He helped to keep the slaves in line—using the Bible instead of the whip. The Bible proved to be more effective in many ways. From the beginning of slavery, the master realized that to hold other men in bondage was a crime. Instead of seeking to end slavery, however, he sought justification for it. Such justification was found in the Bible. Many other people had been enslaved, and for the most part, he concluded, they had been enslaved for their own good. Black people, in particular, were destined to be slaves; they were the descendants of Ham, who was said by God to be "a hewer of wood and a drawer of water."

Many slaves never accepted this justification for their condition. They continued to run away, to poison masters, and to sabotage the operations of the plantations by any means possible. The master, therefore, made the Bible and Christianity serve still another purpose: that of convincing the slave that slavery was beneficial to him; that it was natural, and that if he fulfilled his calling as a slave well—did not run away from his master, did his work conscientiously, never revolted—he would be rewarded in heaven for his "trials and tribulations" on earth. Therefore, the work of the plantation preacher was already cut out for him.

Lucretia Alexander was an ex-slave. In B. A. Botkin's book, *Lay My Burden Down,* she tells of the duties of the preacher: "The [black people] didn't go to the church building; the preacher came and preached to them in their quarters. He'd just say, 'Serve your masters. Don't steal your masters' chickens. Don't steal your masters' hogs. Don't steal your masters' meat. Do whatsoever your master tells you to do.' Same old thing all the time."

Another former slave, Anderson Edwards was a preacher himself. He tells how he came to join the profession and what his duties were. "I had been preaching the gospel and farming since slavery time. I jines the church most 83 years ago when I was Major Gauds slave, and they baptizes me in the spring close to where I finds the lord. When I starts preaching I couldn't read or write and had to preach what the master told me, and he say tell them niggers if 'en they obeys the master they goes to heaven; but I knowed there's something better for them, but daren't tell them except on the sly. That I done lots. I tells em iffen they keeps praying, the lord will set em free."

The master used the teachings of Christianity to keep his slaves content. The Negro preacher was important in this undertaking. If he did his job well, harmony and peace prevailed on the plantation. Many slaves, offered a chance to go to heaven, thought twice about running away to freedom. If a slave believed that the poor were blessed, he thought twice before stealing from his master to add to his own meager rations. If it was true that the meek would inherit the earth, then there was no grace to be attained by killing the master. Under the spell of Christianity, many became resigned to a life of slavery, believing that the institution was right in the eyes of God.

Many, but not all. Nat Turner was a slave who belonged to Joseph Travis. He was born in 1800. Like Anderson Edwards, he was also a minister. Unlike Edwards, however, Turner was able to read and write. He read the Bible and discovered statements that the master never mentioned. They were skipped over by black and white preachers alike. There were such statements as "an eye for an eye," and "do unto others as you would have them do unto you." Moreover, he discovered in the Bible men who were not timid, meek, and forgiving! There was Moses, who had rescued the children of Israel. There was Joshua, who fought a mighty battle at Jericho. There was the one true Christian, who had died on the cross to free all men—he had not told them to accept their slavery. Turner decided that he wanted to be like these men. He wanted to risk his life in order to free his people.

Christianity's effect on him differed from its effect on most other slaves. This can be seen from an account of his actions prior to his rebellion. Herbert Aptheker tells us that in the spring of 1828, while working in the fields, Turner "heard a loud noise in the heavens, and the spirit instantly appeared to me and said the serpent was loosened, and Christ had laid down the yoke he had borne for the sins of men, and that I should take it on and girth against the serpent, for the time was fast approaching when the first should be last and the last should be first."

On August 21, 1831, Nat Turner took up the "yoke." He led six slaves in rebellion. The first to feel the wrath of the minister were his master and his master's family. News of the rebellion spread to surrounding plantations. More and more black people joined the revolt. Soon, seventy men and women were engaged in an attempt to secure freedom.

They made the attempt in the same manner the Israelites had used in freeing themselves from Egyptian bondage. The revolt was soon ended. Turner, the last of the revolutionaries to be captured, was taken alive on October 30th. He was brought to trial in a Virginia court, found guilty and sentenced to die. On November 11th, the slave who had interpreted the Bible in his own way, was hanged by the neck until he was dead.

Matilda would not have wanted her son to be the kind of minister that Nat Turner had been, nor would she have wanted him to be the kind of minister that Edwards had been. Dunbar rebelled against the idea of being any kind of minister at all. He did not want to be trapped in a profession for which he believed he had no calling. He tried not to disappoint his mother; but he made clear to her very early that the ministry was not for him. He was a lover of nature. He loved the open spaces; he was fond of sitting beside clear streams and allowing his pole to dangle as he studied the landscape. Such a man needed the kind of freedom that the office of minister, doctor, or lawyer would not afford.

Dunbar desired freedom from restrictions above all else; as did his fictional counterpart, Freddie Brent. Both were restricted by tradition, and neither thought he could win his fight against "blind fate." By the end of *The Uncalled*, however, Freddie would win his fight, and Dunbar, through identification with his character would win a victory also. As Saunders Redding has noted, Dunbar not only wrote about white characters, he became the white characters about whom he wrote. Paul Laurence Dunbar is Freddie Brent and Freddie Brent is Paul Laurence Dunbar. Freddie is trapped in the town of Dexter; he is forced to obey the dictates of Hester Prime; he attempts to live down his past.

At the time *The Uncalled* was written Dunbar was forced to be the kind of poet he did not want to be; he was forced to obey the dictates of his critics; he, too, was attempting to live down his past.

But unlike Brent, Dunbar did not rebel openly. He confided his disappointment only to friends; he showed his anger in one or two short stories; he wrote of the fate which had befallen him in a score of poems; he made his most eloquent defense against tyranny in *The Uncalled*. However, not once did he broach the subject to his critics, not once did he tell Howells, as he had told others, that the critic had done him "irreparable harm."

He had a number of opportunities. Two months after Howells' review appeared in *Harpers*, Dunbar visited the critic at the latter's home in Far Rockaway, New York. Howells greeted him affectionately, beaming as he spoke: "This is Paul Dunbar! This is Paul Dunbar! . . . Come in, Come in, I'm so happy to see you and meet you personally." The warm greeting was followed by supper and conversation. Howells talked of his days in Dayton, Ohio. He talked about his father's newspaper, which he had worked on and which had been started in Dayton many years before Dunbar was born. He talked about poetry in general, and admonished the young poet to "write more dialect pieces—they're your contribution to American letters." When the visit was over and Dunbar was about to leave, a late summer rain had begun. The critic offered the use of his raincoat. This act of generosity, coming from so renowned a man, was something the poet never forgot.

He never forgot his hostility to Howells' evaluation of his poetic talents either. Yet on no occasion did he make these known to Howells. He suffered in private and hoped that such novels as *The Uncalled* would so captivate his public,

as to reveal all critics as false prophets. The public, however, did not like *The Uncalled*. The book was said to be
too romantic, to be lacking in local color, to be filled with
improbable events, and to be of a mediocre quality. The
reviewers were partially right. *The Uncalled* fails as a novel
because the events are unrealistic; for example, Freddie's
accidental encounter with his father at the temperance
meeting. In addition, the language is artificial and the characters are romanticized. However, these are the reasons
for the failure of Dunbar's fiction in general. The collections
of short stories, *The Strength of Gideon*, *Folks from Dixie*,
and *In Old Plantation Days* all fail for the same reasons:
none is true to life, the situations in each are implausible,
the language is artificial, and the characters are way outside
the range of possibility.

Folks from Dixie consisted of twelve short stories, and
with the exception of "At Shaft 11," each deals with an aspect of the plantation tradition. "At Shaft 11," which tells
of a labor strike in a coal-mining town, and "Jimsella," the
story of a young married couple, who after leaving the
South encounter great difficulty in the North, are the only
two stories in the volume that contain elements of reality.

"Anner 'Lizer's Stumblin' Block," the lead story in the collection, deals with religion on the plantation. Anner 'Lizer
seeks the true religion. However, Sam, her fiance, is a sinner. He would rather go "possum huntin'" on Sunday than
attend church services. Anner 'Lizer is attempting to be
converted; she wants to receive the Holy Ghost. Dunbar's
description of the religious ceremony in which Anner 'Lizer
tries to get the spirit, owes more to Methodism as practiced
by the eighteenth-century preacher John Wesley than to
the religion taught on the plantation. In Dunbar's depiction, there is a great deal of breast beating and loud chant-

ing; the penitent catches the spirit, jumps up and down, and shakes himself into a state of insensibility before falling to his knees.

Anner 'Lizer is constantly exhorted by the preacher: "De Lawd is jes on de othah side; jes one step away, waitin to receibe you. Wont you come to him? Wont you tek de chance o becomin j'int 'ars o dat beautiful city whar de streets is gold an de gates is pearly? Wont you come to him sinnah? Dont you see de pityin look he's a-givin you, a-sayin' 'Come, Come.'"

Try as she may, however, the sinner cannot "come through." Whenever she approaches the moment of conversion, she thinks of Sam and the spirit flees. Sam goes on about the business of coon hunting. He has no idea of Anner 'Lizer's terrible ordeal. One evening the two meet by accident. Anner 'Lizer has gone out alone to wrestle with her soul in private. Sam is examining the springs on his traps. When the two meet, he promises to marry the distraught girl. "The same night," Dunbar tells us, "the minister announced 'dat de Lawd had found out de sistah's stumblin block an removed it f'om de path.'"

"The Colonel's Awakening" and "The Intervention of Peter" are more in the vein of white writers of the plantation tradition. Both stories deal with the loyalty of slaves in the old South. In "The Colonel's Awakening," two slaves, Ike and Lize, remain on the plantation after the Civil War in order to care for their former master, Colonel Robert Estridge. Dunbar describes the colonel as one for whom ". . . time had not passed and conditions had not changed from a generation. He was still the gallant aristocrat he had been when the war broke out—a little past the age to enlist himself, but able and glad to give two sons to the cause of the South."

The colonel lives in the past. Although his sons died in the Civil War, he still awaits their return. He believes that his plantation is as prosperous as it was previously, and he is ignorant of the change that has come over the South and the nation. The faithful servants help to keep his vision alive. They continue to perform as they had done in the old days. They attend to his personal comfort; they do the chores that had once been done by hundreds of slaves in an attempt to keep the plantation from running down; they humor him when he makes remarks anticipating the return of his sons; they give him the same Christmas present each year that a neighbor, Miss Randolph, had given him. Each year, the neighbor, long since passed away, had knitted the old man a pair of gloves. However, this year Lize decides to "make him somep'n' diffunt." She knits a comforter to go around his neck. The change of presents shocks the old man back to sanity. Later in the day, the two slaves find him dead. Near his body are many pairs of gloves, and clasped in his hand is the last pair that Miss Randolph knitted before her death.

In "The Intervention of Peter," a loyal slave intervenes in a duel between his master Harrison Randolph and a former friend, Bob Lee. The two men, "gentlemen of Virginia's finest families" have a quarrel during which Lee insults Randolph, who demands an apology. When Lee refuses, the time and place for the duel is set. Peter is apprehensive about the welfare of his master. On the morning of the duel, he goes to the site where the duel is to take place and conceals himself behind a ledge with an "ancient fowling piece." Just before the duel begins Peter aims the gun at Bob Lee. Before the gun goes off he is discovered, and makes the following confession: "I was gwine ti fiah jes befo dey said free. I wasnt gwine to kill you, Mas Bob. I was ony gwine to lame you." The sight of the slave with the broken gun causes both men to laugh convulsively. The duel is forgotten, the two men shake hands, and Peter is congratulated for having saved the day.

With few exceptions, the rest of the stories in *Folks from Dixie* show variations on the themes of black loyalty to white people, dedication to the South, and fondness for the "old way of life." There is no cry for freedom to be found in these stories; there is no attempt by the author to concern himself with reality. The stories fabricate events and, in general, "give the lie to truth." The reader is led to believe that these people from Dixie are happy, content, and have no worries or cares. Their feelings about white people are crudely distorted, as Ike's speech in "The Colonel's Awakening" shows: "I do' know whut I'd do ef I didn't have Mas' Bob to wuk fu'." Distortions or no, such sentiments were more pleasing to whites than those expressing the desire for freedom. The nation wanted one picture and one picture only of black men, and like many black writers both past and present, Dunbar felt obliged to acquiesce to those wishes.

"The author," writes Benjamin Brawley, "was working as a practical craftsman, and he knew what would be approved by the editors of the day and what would not." It is to Dunbar's credit that he continued to write things—though very few—that would not be approved by the editors. However *Folks from Dixie* increased his fame, *The Uncalled* did not. After the former, his popularity soared, his reputation was firmly established, and his financial situation improved to the point that he decided to try to earn his living by his pen alone.

Fifteen months after taking the job as a clerk in the Library of Congress, he began to feel stifled. At first, the job had intrigued him. He was a lover of books, and he delighted in being among so many famous authors of the past. If these poets were alive today, what would be their judgment of him? They, themselves, had been judged by history. To some of them, history had been kind; to others, brutal. Yet, those who wrote history were seldom poets. Perhaps a poet should be judged by other poets and what better judgment could he receive than judgment by these ancient poets?

However, there were duties to perform, which had nothing to do with holding communion with the dead. In one of the library's many rooms, he gave daily readings for children. These were some of the most enjoyable hours of his working day. He liked to watch the children. They stamped their feet in time to the rhythm of the poem as he read, laughed at the humorous ditties, and sometimes repeated lines and verses after him in their childish voices. They helped to make his time at the library more pleasant than it might have been otherwise. For there were unpleasant moments. There were times when he was alone with his thoughts about himself. Perhaps he would not have wanted his fellow poets to judge him after all. Their judgment would have been as harsh as his own; and perhaps it was better not to have an echo repeating the censure that one gave oneself.

There was one such moment when, despondent, he sat looking at the iron gratings around one of the book stacks. He thought of a bird's cage. How would it feel to be a bird, imprisoned behind those bars? The bird would not be able to fly or to free himself through his own power. He would be trapped. How analogous the situation of such a bird to his own! He was trapped in this thing some men called fame, which more sensitive men called madness. He, also, was incapable of extricating himself. In a sense, he and the bird were one, just as he and Freddie Brent were one.

Freddie Brent would have understood the bird. Like the poet, he would have immortalized his feelings in lines of enduring beauty.

Dunbar felt a profound sense of pity and deep sympathy for the bird, caught in a cage from which there was no escape. But he was also proud of it because the bird did not take its captivity passively. It beat its wings against the cage until they were bloody, in a vain attempt to escape. The world would not share Dunbar's sympathy. It would continue to look upon the bird with condescension: wondering why it would pain itself to be free; not believing the bars to be a prison, but rather a home—a place where all birds belong. This was, as the poet knew, because few would ever attempt to imagine how the caged bird felt.

VII

A TERRIBLE, LONE, STILL FIGHT

When Foes upon me press, let me not quail,
Nor think to turn me into coward flight.
I only ask to make mine arm prevail,
Strength for the fight.

It was April of 1899 and William Dean Howells, now sixty-two years old, made his way slowly up a long flight of stairs. The stairs were located in a shabby, run-down, New York City apartment building. In one of the apartments, on a neat bed with clean white sheets, the "poet laureate of the Negro race" lay close to death. Howells was one of the many who came to the sick bed of the young poet during those two terrible weeks in April when he wrestled with pneumonia.

Letters of concern came from every state in the nation. Men from the highest stations of life made daily inquiries or sent emissaries to visit him. People whom the poet had never seen flooded his room with flowers. Prayers were said for him in churches of every major denomination. As he lay near death, the newspapers ran daily reports on his condition. The first report labeled his condition critical.

The illness had begun slowly. During his fifteen-month stay at the Library of Congress, dust from the old manuscripts of books, magazines, and newspapers had begun to accumulate in his lungs. As he continued his hectic schedule, work and time combined to transform a slight annoyance into something much more serious. In Boston, one week before falling ill, he had written to a friend: "My readings here have been successful, the one at Hollis Street Theatre being quite a triumph. But they have been a little too much for me, and I am now suffering from a cold, fatigue, and a bad throat."

He did not want to give up his readings. They provided a supplement to his income. Moreover, he loved to read his poetry aloud. He was a good reader, and he was often thrilled at the applause and appreciation he received from his audiences. He had begun to give readings while still a student at Central High School—reading poetry before his classmates—and after this, he had read before his neighbors. He discovered, after the publication of *Oak and Ivy*, that readings were a means of introducing people to his book. Therefore, he stepped up the pace. Few of the engagements during these early years paid very well; some paid nothing at all. However, as he became better known, the readings contributed substantially to his income.

He left the Library at the beginning of the year. From that time until his illness, he filled over one hundred engagements. The engagement at the Hollis Theatre had been one of his last. In Boston, preparing for this engagement, he had stayed with Alice's parents. The Moores had rented a cabin for the summer outside of Boston, and they welcomed their son-in-law warmly. The past antagonisms had disappeared. They had resigned themselves to their daughter's choice. Moreover, they had reason to believe that her choice was not as dreadful as they had once thought it to be. The nation continued to applaud their son-in-law, continued to heap laurels upon his head.

Everywhere they went, they encountered some mention

of the name of Paul Laurence Dunbar. Invariably, their daughter was also mentioned, as if it were unthinkable to mention one without the other. They arrived at the conclusion that the two young people needed each other. Like Dunbar's friends, they realized that without Alice the poet might have fallen along the wayside long ago. This was not only because he was very delicate and sensitive, but also because he was not very practical. The world demanded a great deal of him. If left alone, he would have attempted to satisfy every demand that the world made. Therefore, Alice was more than just a wife—she was also an astute business manager. She selected his readings, choosing those from which he would profit most in terms of money and prestige. She suggested the benefits at which he should appear and those he should politely refuse. She advised him concerning causes to which he was asked to lend his name—distinguishing those that would enhance his prestige from those that might injure his reputation.

Alice needed her husband also! She was strong-willed and impulsive, and yet she longed for acts of tenderness and understanding. She needed someone who could fulfill these needs, someone whose fidelity to nature and a free and uncomplicated existence was as strong as hers. Like her husband, Alice Dunbar underwent a private struggle against rigidity and confinement; and her struggle was equally intense. Also like Dunbar, she sought escape in literature, creating for herself a world in which the darkness of night entered only at one's own invitation.

In 1894 she published a series of short stories entitled *Violets and Other Tales* in the *Boston Monthly Review*. In 1899 Dodd, Mead & Company published her *The Goodness of St. Rocque*. The titles of these volumes reveal an important aspect of her character. She was a romantic, a dreamer—one who escaped from the horrors of the world by finding refuge in the things of nature. One finds in *Sonnet*, one of her many uncollected poems, the idea of a union between man and nature:

> *I had no thought of violets of late,*
> *The wild, shy kind that spring beneath your feet*
> *In wistful April days, when lovers mate*
> *And wander through the fields in raptures sweet.*

To one who had lost such thoughts due to despair, the thought of violets caused her to think at first not of nature or even love, but instead of ". . . florist's shops,/And bow and pins, and perfumed papers fine;/And garish lights, and mincing little fops/And cabarets and songs, and deadening wine." Yet, for her, these were not real things:

> *So far from sweet real things my thoughts had strayed,*
> *I had forgot wide fields, and clear brown streams.*

Because these were "the things of nature," for Alice Dunbar, they were also the things of reality. According to the poem, only when the lover can bring to his beloved a sense of these things—a part of earth, flowers and trees—then, and only then, can the violet become what it was born to be— a link between two lovers that joins both to nature. Her religious commitment to nature bordered upon a paranoiac obsession with innocence. She was one of the most sophisticated of women; yet, the things that brought her joy were children and the types of tales that children tend to love, poetry which spoke of violets and seas, and a husband who knew how to "enjoy a day among the leaves." There was a contradiction between her practicality and the romanticism that was too strong for her to bear. It may have been this contradiction that sometime later would force her to view her marriage as no longer innocent, the love between herself and her husband as no longer cemented by the violet.

These were not the thoughts of March. The two lay together, fishing on Boston's Mystic River. From time to time, Alice's mother appeared with sandwiches and other refreshments. Alice's niece, Lelia, hovered constantly around the poet, never allowing him to stray far from her side. The March wind became raw and blustery and the clouds darkened overhead. Dunbar remained at his pole. He anxiously watched the bobbing, weaving cork; the bait line swayed and moved, due to the force of the wind. Once he almost caught a fish, or thought he did. Something tugged at his line; however, when he snatched the line from the water, both bait and fish were gone. He continued to sit on the bank of the river. Finally, when he began to shiver from the cold, he went empty-handed back to the house. The next day he prepared to leave for engagements in Philadelphia and New York.

He had a rasping cold. His throat felt like raw flesh. Slight chills wracked his body and his temperature rose. He drank hot liquids for breakfast and prepared to depart. Alice was about to return to Washington. She was concerned about him, but he insisted that he had nothing more than "a little cold." He was determined to keep his engagements. He had given his word, and never before had he failed to honor it. In addition, *Lyrics of the Hearthside* had recently been released, and his presence was necessary to help publicize the book.

Lyrics of the Hearthside, dedicated to Alice, was released in February of 1899. This was his second book of poetry to be published by Dodd, Mead & Company. The format of the book differed from that of *Lyrics of Lowly Life* in that the dialect poems and those in standard English were separated from each other as they had been in the earlier books, *Oak and Ivy,* and *Majors and Minors.* The desperate struggle he waged with his own spirit—against a world he dared to fight openly—is here revealed more clearly than in the previous volumes. Here, in lines that tell of love, joy, melancholia, struggle, and death, is the stuff of his life, his inner-self, the material of his poetic essence. Of all these themes, he began to write most frequently of death. This was not a new theme for him. He had written of death, of the end of life, in *Oak and Ivy, Majors and Minors* and *Lyrics of Lowly Life.* However, for the most part, these poems had merely been speculations about death—youthful investigations of a world that attracts because it is unknown.

Now, his statements on death took on a maturity of form. He wrote of it with a passion and an understanding peculiar for a young man of twenty-seven. Death was still unknowable. Yet he looked upon it now as not being very far away, a mystery soon to be a mystery no more, the unknowable destined eventually to make itself known. Even in the love poems there is this longing for escape, for release from the earthly pain that only death can bring. No volume of his works is more despondent than *Lyrics of the Hearthside;* no lines appear in any of his other writings so filled with resignation and despair. It was as though he were prophesying the day yet to come: preparing himself for the fall that the morrow would bring, resigning himself to that fate over which he had no control.

Lyrics of the Hearthside opens with *Love's Apotheosis*. In this poem the speaker addresses a plea to his loved one:

> *Love me. I care not what the circling years*
> > *To me may do.*
> *If, but in spite of time and tears,*
> > *You prove but true.*

The plea continues and grows more insistent, stanza by stanza. In each stanza the poet names those afflictions that might befall him. There is grief, which dims the eyes; winter snow with chills of age, pain, and care. The poet concludes by asking his beloved to lessen the impact of these dreaded afflictions by remaining true: "Love me, and let my life take up thine own."

That this poem should begin a book dedicated to Alice is not surprising. Nor is it surprising that the speaker appeals to his love to remain with him forever, through periods of darkness and pain as well as those of sunshine and light—for the book was written during a time when the poet's life was a mixture of both. *Lyrics of the Hearthside* is the "fruitage" of the years spent wrestling with his conscience after Howells' review, of his experiences in England, and of the uncertainty concerning his marriage. At that time he had needed a love such as that called for in *Love's Apotheosis*, and there is little doubt that Alice fulfilled that need.

This belief that love might act as a barrier between him and the world is found in other poems in this volume. At times he seems to conceive of love as being more than emotion, more even than a bond between two human beings. With the world closing in on him, out of despair, he makes love an instrument—sometimes even a weapon—to be used in combating his many enemies. It is this sense of love as weapon that one finds in the poem, *Love's Phases:*

> *Love hath the wings of the eagle bold,*
>   *Cling to him strongly—*
> *What if the look of the world be cold,*
>   *And life go wrongly?*
> *Rest on his pinions, for broad is their fold;*
>   *Love hath the wings of the eagle bold.*
>
> *Love hath the voice of the storm at night,*
>   *Wildly defiant.*
> *Hear him and yield up your soul to his might,*
>   *Tenderly pliant.*
> *None shall regret him who heed him aright;*
>   *Love hath the voice of the storm at night.*

Yet he had only admiration for those who met the challenge of life head on. He pays tribute to Harriet Beecher Stowe who ". . . told the story,/And the whole world wept /At wrongs and cruelties it had not known/But for this fearless woman's voice alone." In a poem in memory of Alexander Crummell, the Negro leader who had once befriended him, what begins as a tribute becomes a mirror of the poet's own pessimism concerning the fate of his people.

> *Back to the breast of thy mother,*
> *Child of the earth!*
> *E'en her caress can not smother*
> *What thou hast done. . . .*
> *Unto a nation whose sky was as night,*
> *Camest thou, holily, bearing thy light:*

In the last stanza, the poet advises his dead friend:

> *Back to the breast of thy mother—*
> *To rest.*
> *Long hast thou striven;*
> *Dared where the hills by the lightening of*
> *heaven were riven;*
> *Go now, pure shriven.*

There was the question:

> *Who shall come after thee, out of the clay—*
> *Learned one and leader to show us the way?*
> *Who shall rise up when the world gives*
> *the test?*

and the advice:

> *Think thou no more of this—*
> *Rest!*

However, the poems that stand out in the first part of the book are those in which the poet looks at death through older eyes. The most beautiful, and perhaps the saddest of all his poems, is *When All Is Done*. It is also the most personal. Here, more than anywhere else, the poet poured pain, anguish, despair, and heartbreak into one loud, long wail for the release which only death could bring:

> *When all is done, and my last word is said,*
> *And ye who loved me murmur, 'He is dead,'*
> *Let no one weep, for fear that I should know,*
> *And sorrow too that ye should sorrow so.*

When all is done and in the oozing clay,
Ye lay this cast-off hull of mine away,
Pray not for me, for, after long despair,
The quiet of the grave will be a prayer.

For I have suffered loss and grievous pain,
The hurts of hatred and the world's disdain,
And wounds so deep, that love, well-tried and pure,
Had not the pow'r to ease them or to cure.

And, in the final stanza, the infatuation with death is complete:

When all is done, say not my day is o'er,
And that thro' night I seek a dimmer shore:
Say rather that my morn has just begun,—
I greet the dawn and not a setting sun,
   When all is done.

Beside such poems as these, those in dialect are mere ornament. Yet, here, in this book, are included some of Dunbar's most popular dialect poetry: *Little Brown Baby, Angelina, Whistling Sam, At Candle-Lightin' Time, Temptation,* and *How Lucy Backslid.* However, not even the dialect poetry was free of the theme of death:

   Lay me down beneaf de willers in de grass,
   Whah de branch'll go a-singin' as it pass.
      An w'en I's a-layin' low,
      I kin hyeah it as it go,
   Singin', "Sleep, my honey, tek yo res'
      at las'."

Now he lay near death. The cold and fatigue he had

written about turned into pneumonia. As he left Boston for New York, the symptoms became more visible. The cough bothered him throughout his readings; yet he continued. He made plans to return to New York in April when his poem, *The Deserted Plantation*—put to music by the composer Walter Damrosch—would be included in a program to be given at the Waldorf Astoria. A week later, he planned to appear at a reading in New York at which he was to be introduced by Governor Theodore Roosevelt. These engagements lay ahead. At the moment there were previously made promises to be kept in the Midwest, and he hastened to honor them.

Spring came late to the Midwest in 1899. Frost and snow remained on the ground throughout the month of May. Wherever the poet went the chill wind added to his discomfort. His cold became progressively worse. The fever came, left, and came again. It was difficult for him to find enough clothes or bedding to warm the chill that caused his frail body to shake and tremble. Drugstore medicines proved to be ineffective against the infection, which had now almost taken control of his body.

Arriving in New York on the day of the reading, he nearly collapsed. Mrs. Matthews, who had given the going-away party in his honor before he left for England, talked the reluctant poet into going to bed. She called a doctor. The doctor's report was grave: high fever, heavy chest coughs, and pain—advanced pneumonia. He was too ill to be moved to a hospital. He must remain at Mrs. Matthews'. Alice was sent for and she boarded the earliest train from Washington to New York.

There was not enough room at the Matthews' home for his mother, so Mrs. Dunbar was forced to wait—as the world waited—and receive reports of her son's progress through the same media. Daily, like millions throughout the country, she followed the news of his illness through the newspapers. One day the papers reported that he was holding his own; the next day, that he had gotten progressively worse. On the following day the news was that he had rallied again, and so on and on. For two weeks the accounts wavered between the poles of progress and relapse. At the end of the third week, more optimistic bulletins began to appear. His recovery was hinted at, although no one would venture to say so openly. After a month, his name all but disappeared from the tabloids. He had rallied; he had won the fight against death.

The struggle had been a long and costly one. It left him permanently impaired. His lungs were infected. He might fall prey to another attack immediately unless he rested for at least six months in a dry, mountainous climate. Alice began to search for a place suitable for his recuperation. In making her choice, she would have to bear many factors in mind. The climate must not be too hot or too cold; neither too humid nor too dry. In addition, there was the problem of choosing something that they could afford. She chose the Catskill Mountains in upstate New York.

To get the poet to the Catskills was easy, to get him to rest was extremely difficult. There were contracts to be filled—knowing that he had survived, his public did not ask under what conditions. They wanted entertainment from his pen once again, and he sought to oblige them. There were reasons other than the appeasement of his public. It was doubtful now that he would be able to continue giving readings. At any rate, it would be impossible for him to read on the average of six or seven times a week as he had previously done. Yet these readings had contributed to his income. Without them, how would he be able to support his wife and mother?

True, his books were doing well. Yet he knew that the income of a writer was not guaranteed, especially when it depended upon the whims of a frivolous public. The only possible solution was to fulfill as many of the contracts as possible. Therefore, he wrote poems, short stories, and articles as if his illness had never occurred. At times Alice was successful in persuading him to go fishing. At other times, he pleaded the pressure of work. A boyhood friend, Dr. Robert Burns, took the poet under his care. Refusing to take no for an answer, Dr. Burns insisted that a large part of each day be given over to boating, fishing, and picnicking.

Dunbar's strength began to return. He regained some of his lost weight. Always thin, his weight was between one hundred and twenty-five and one hundred and thirty-five pounds when he was in the best of health. Due to his illness, his weight had fallen close to the one hundred mark. His appetite grew strong once again. The laugh came back to his eyes and face. Fond of dancing, he would waltz his wife around the floor of the little bungalow, sometimes pausing because of shortness of breath, but always finishing out his dance and ending by kissing her on the cheek.

Yet, he was still a sick man. The pain had not left his chest. At night, it frequently became so unbearable that he could not sleep. To ease the pain, he began to drink. At first he drank small shots of bourbon. As the pain increased, so did the amount of alcohol. In the fall, having planned a return to Washington, he visited his doctor once again. The news was not encouraging. His lungs had not healed satisfactorily. The doctor advised him to go to Colorado and remain throughout the winter. The prescription was six months in a high, dry climate.

Once again, unexpectedly, plans had to be made. In order for his mother to accompany him and his wife, the house in Washington had to be sold. Money was needed in greater amounts than he possessed. He had no means of acquiring these additional funds and therefore began to seek writing assignments. The arguments with which he had previously engaged himself ceased. He now needed his audience more than his audience needed him. Fate, that phenomenon which determines men's lives and of which he had written in *The Uncalled,* had now taken hold of the reins of his life in the most terrible of all possible ways—making him a poet for hire.

At first, he had wanted a hearing—he had wanted people to listen to what he had to say—and for this reason he had begun to write dialect verse. Later, when they would listen to nothing else, he continued to write dialect poetry. Yet he did so with the knowledge that he was forced to and, therefore, was not being poetically dishonest. Now, he realized that he was cashing in on his reputation—bargaining away the last part of his individual soul. Is it any wonder that his consumption of liquor increased?

There were willing arms to fly into, and he flew into them. George Lorimer, editor of the *Saturday Evening Post,* wanted a series of stories based on some of his most famous plantation tradition characters: Aunt Tempy, Aunt Joshy, and Uncle Ike. *Lippincott* wanted a light novel. The Denver *Post* offered him an assignment as a roving reporter. Other magazines and newspapers responded with requests for poems, articles, and short stories. He accepted all but one. The assignment by the Denver *Post* would have been too taxing. If he were involved in traveling from one part of Colorado to another, he would have little time to rest or work on his other projects. However, the editor amended the offer and made it more attractive: he could do only those assignments he wanted to do. In addition, the paper would bear the expenses incurred by Dunbar and his wife in settling in Colorado. The business arrangements concluded, the three left for Colorado in September. About the first of October, they took up residence in Harmon, a small town outside of Denver.

Their new home was small but comfortable. Once again the poet began the long trip toward recovery. Under the care of his wife and mother, he began to show signs of improvement. He was able to exercise, and although he still suffered from shortness of breath, breathing after exercise was becoming easier. He wrote as much as before. In addition to poems and articles, he worked on a collection of stories and a novel. He began to give readings again, though less frequently than before.

Friends from the West stopped in to visit him. Among these were Sissieretta Jones, the singer, and Booker T. Washington. He attracted the attention of Major William Cooke, a young businessman from Denver, to whom he dedicated *The Love of Landry*. Cooke was eager to ingratiate himself with a famous literary personality. He offered Dunbar the run of his large estate and the loan of his extensive library. However, the poet wanted to be alone and eventually terminated the relationship with his young admirer.

The truth was that he missed the East. He missed being somewhat free to roam, to chart out his own path. Once again, like the bird he imagined to be imprisoned in its cage, he too was being locked in; his freedom was being denied. He sometimes wished that he could rip the diseased lungs from his chest, that he could find another way of breathing—one which would not tie him down like an invalid. He became more and more disagreeable, harder and harder to please. The pain reappeared at short intervals, each spasm reminding him that he was a slave to a diseased body. He wrote to a friend: "I still have hopes of coming East in the spring, but the doctors discourage me about its being a permament stay there; so I shall probably stop a short time in Washington and go thence to the Catskills . . . I am not so well now as I was at first, though my breathing is somewhat better . . ."

As he looked forward to the spring and the trip back East, he worked diligently on the novel, *The Love of Landry*. The editor had asked for "a light novel," and this book filled the bill. It was a love story and took place in Colorado. Mildred, the heroine, comes West to regain her health. There she meets and falls in love with a cowboy named Landry. However, the affair is opposed by one of Mildred's relatives, Aunt Annesley, who lives in the East. During a cattle stampede, the heroine is saved by Landry. For this act, he wins her hand. She is cured and finds both happiness and health.

Once again, despite such a slight plot, Dunbar manages to impose his personal experiences on the novel. Each of the major characters represents some aspect of Dunbar's experiences: Arthur Heathclift, the English suitor for the hand of the heroine, a man who "smells of civilization," is a character modeled after Englishmen whom the poet had met during his stay in England. Heathclift is, to be sure, a poor stereotype of an Englishman, yet he represents Dunbar's idea of a civilized man. John Osborne is the kind, considerate father. He reminds one of the equally kind and considerate Doctor Tobey. Dunbar cherished Tobey's friendship as small boys cherish their relationship with their fathers. There is Aunt Annesley who attempts to interfere in the romance between Landry and Mildred, just as Alice's parents had attempted to interfere in their romance. Mildred, the heroine, suffers from tuberculosis. Like Dunbar, she is forced to come to Colorado to regain her health. Landry Thaler whose name, Landry, reminds one of land, is a man of the earth. Once a part of the frustration and chaos of the city, he has forsaken urban America and come back to nature. With such characters—each symbolizing different aspects of his character—Dunbar wrote a novel in which he, once again, deals with the theme of personal freedom.

Like the characters in his first novel, *The Uncalled,* the characters in his second novel are also white. However, where Freddie Brent, the hero of *The Uncalled,* sought freedom from the iron grip of Hester Prime, Mildred and Landry, heroine and hero of *The Love of Landry,* seek freedom from the civilized world. The novel depicts a conflict between the civilized world and the world of nature: "Nothing," the author states in the novel, "is quite so conceited as what we call civilization. And what does it mean after all except to lie gracefully, to cheat legally and to live as far away from God and nature as the world limit will allow."

The battle between civilization and nature is undertaken by Heathclift and Landry. Heathclift represents civilized man; Landry, natural man. Mildred must choose between the two. The choice is as much Dunbar's as it is Mildred's. He was a small-town boy who had always been suspicious of the city. Now, however, he had come to hate it. His hatred was intense, like that of one who has spent all of his life in the woods. He disliked the city's impersonality, its coldness, its bigness. He interpreted these characteristics in terms of sin, corruption, and evil. The city strangled everything in its midst. It trapped one in its gaudiness, its wildness. It was composed of cold streets without trees or grass; its boys became hardened men—hardened to the point of becoming prisoners of themselves. They were, in other words, cynical men who dedicated their lives to the world of reality.

On the other hand, now confined by tuberculosis, *his* only freedom lay in the realm of dreams. Therefore, he scorned men for whom reality was more important than the dream. He was alone a great deal of the time and was forced to look into himself. He became openly contemptuous of situations in which men were forced to live in the midst of crowds, their destinies dictated by external forces. In Mildred, he manufactured joy. He made her young, frivolous, and carefree—all that he would have liked to become.

Landry possessed sufficient strength to turn his back on civilization, to say no to fortune. He made the choice between the dream world and the real world, between the natural world and the civilized world. He threw off the "yoke of civilization," followed his own impulses and became a free man. The land was his salvation; it dictated commands not to his head, but to his heart. His laughter was not artificial; his joy was not manufactured. His sense of being one with all humanity came spontaneously as though he constantly communed with the world of God.

Nature could be mastered—its world could be subdued in a way that the world of man could not. The most exciting chapter in *The Love of Landry* is devoted to the cattle stampede during which Landry rescues Mildred. Dunbar had spent hours with Major Cooke listening to the Coloradan relate stories of cattle stampedes. He learned how they began, what it was like to hear the fury of the hoofs of thousands of cattle pounding the earth and how the earth shook under the impact, how the cattle seemed wild, carefree, demoniacal as they surged forward, running wildly in all directions—free, vibrant, uninhibited.

Therefore, when he placed Landry in the midst of this— nature's thunderous revolt—Dunbar made him a hero, one whom he himself would have liked to emulate. Landry challenged the forces of nature and mastered them. Dunbar had previously wanted to be like Freddie Brent; now he wanted to be like Landry. Freddie had managed to break away from Hester Prime, from religious bigotry and tradition. He had made a new life for himself, free from restrictions. However, Freddie Brent did not go all the way. His emancipation did not result in his returning to the earth. He continued to struggle in the world of men, attempting to exercise his freedom in that world.

When he wrote *The Uncalled*, Dunbar had sought a hearing. He had hoped that his fellow men would understand his veiled plea for artistic freedom, that they would agree with him that the poet must be free of restraints. He was experiencing the first light of fame; the world eagerly lent its eyes and ears to him. He had looked at the world through eyes conditioned by the bright glare of publicity; and he had been optimistic even though he was continually plagued with despondency and despair.

When he wrote *The Love of Landry* he had already ended his romance with the world of men. "I am tired, so tired of dialect," he had written. "I send out graceful little poems, suited for any of the magazines, but they are returned to me by editors who say, 'we would be very glad to have a dialect poem, Mr. Dunbar, but we do not care for the language compositions.'" In a letter to his friend Taylor, young Freddie Brent articulates Dunbar's feelings about his dialect poems. One has only to substitute the "poem" for "sermon" and "dialect poet" for "preacher" to realize that the letter tells us as much about Dunbar as it does about Freddie Brent: "It seems to me that one sermon forged a chain which holds me in a position that I hate. It is a public declaration that I am or mean to be a preacher, and I must either adhere to it or break desperately away. Do you know, I feel myself to be an errant coward. If I had half the strength that you have, I should have been out of it long ago; but the habit of obedience grows strong upon a man."

Speaking as the narrator, Dunbar begins Chapter X with these words: "When fate is fighting with all her might against a human soul, the greatest victory that the soul can win is to reconcile itself to the unpleasant, which is never so unpleasant afterwards." When Dunbar became confined to a bungalow in Colorado, he resigned himself to the unpleasant. Yet, he resigned himself to something more. He resigned himself to death. The poet within him was already close to death. Now the body of the poet was dying also. James Weldon Johnson, a friend and fellow poet, recalls a conversation with Dunbar, a few years before his death. "He said to me then," Johnson relates, "'I have not grown. I am writing the same things I wrote ten years ago, and am writing them no better.' His self accusation," adds Johnson, "was not true; he had grown, and he had gained a surer control of his art, but he had not accomplished the greater things of which he was constantly dreaming; the public had held him to the things for which it had accorded him recognition. If Dunbar had lived he would have achieved some of those dreams, but even while he talked so dejectedly to me, he seemed to feel that he was not to live."

Anticipating death—perhaps even with an unconscious wish for it—is there any reason to be surprised that he should imagine himself to be the healthy, physically vibrant, psychologically free Landry Thaler? When Landry throws himself into the midst of thousands of enraged cattle, he throws himself into the face of death with reckless abandon. Since he has mastered the world, it no longer threatens him. Only death threatens him, and Landry takes on this dreaded foe and wins. Dunbar did not believe that he could win. However, like Landry, he had ceased to be afraid of what the long night of "easeful sleep" might mean; he had ceased to be awed by the mystery of it all. The peace that he sought in life, the freedom, came only when he created out of a sense of reality as he knew it, when he created in his white characters images of himself. *The Love of Landry* is a poor novel. But as the account of a poetic spirit seeking escape, seeking release from the bars and cages of life, of a dying soul attempting to lessen the impact of pain upon the still living, it is a remarkable accomplishment.

The Strength of Gideon and Other Stories, with few exceptions, is not remarkable, although this second book of short stories is an improvement over the first. The improvement is due to the fact that Dunbar went beyond the plantation tradition and dealt with material about which he had firsthand information. In moving outside of the plantation tradition, he dealt with aspects of his own personal problems, and one story, "One Man's Fortune" is as close to an autobiography in the short story genre as Dunbar ever came.

There is no hint of a shift, however, in the opening story of the book. "The Strength of Gideon," the title story, tells of the loyalty of the slave Gideon to his master during slavery and to his master's family after the abolition of slavery. Gideon had been loyal and effective as a worker, and for those reasons he was elevated from the field to the big house. He became the master's personal servant and gained the master's confidence. When war broke out between the states, the master entrusted Gideon with the care of his family. "I want you to help your young Mas' Dud look after his mother and Miss Ellen," commanded the master. "You hear? Now that's the one promise I ask of you—come what may, look after the women folks."

Gideon devoted himself to this task. Neither the master nor his son survived the war. Gideon, however, faithful to his word, took control of the plantation and ran it in the interest of his mistress. Nothing could sway him from this task—not even his engagement to Martha, a childhood sweetheart. Martha was obsessed with the idea of freedom. She looked forward to the coming emancipation as a "halleluha day." When the soldiers occupied the town and freed the slaves, she implored Gideon to leave with them. "Gidjon," she said, "I'se waited a long while now. Mos eve'ybody else is gone. Aint you goin?"

"No."

"But Gidjon, I wants to be free. I know how good dey've been to us; but, oh, I wants to own myself. They're talkin 'bout settin us free every hour."

"I can wait."

"They's a camp right near here."

"I promised."

"The of'cers wants body-servants, Gidjon—"

"Go, Martha, if you want to, but I stay."

Martha found such stubbornness as difficult to believe as did most blacks who read the story. She informed the captain of the Union Regiment that there was an excellent body-servant remaining on one of the plantations. The captain went personally to ask Gideon to desert the plantation and offered him a substantial salary to become his personal body-servant. Gideon turned down the offer. The captain made a second offer with a larger salary than the first. Gideon remained adamant. He refused to leave his position as protector of his former master's family.

Martha decides to make one more appeal to Gideon before leaving with the Union troops. When this appeal also falls on deaf ears, she joins the other slaves who were, like herself, drunk with the anticipation of freedom. Gideon watches them leave. Dunbar, paying his debt to the plantation tradition, describes the scene: "He drew out a pace after the troops, and then, turning, looked back at the house. He went a step farther and then a woman's gentle voice called him, 'Gideon.' He crushed his cap in his hands, and the tears came into his eyes. Then, he answered, 'Yes, Miss Ellen, I'se a comin.'"

"The Strength of Gideon," was calculated to please his white audience, as was the second selection, "Mammy Peggy's Pride." Characters like Mammy Peggy are the heroines of Southern folklore. They are as popular with the American mind as Uncle Tom and Uncle Remus. They are the women who ran the big houses for the mistresses and masters. Often, despite their position as slaves, they dominated both master and mistress alike. Like the Gideons, their loyalty to their masters is unshakable and like the Peters, the maladies which afflict the masters afflict them two-fold.

Mammy Peggy was such a character. Of the proud Harrison family and its plantation, all that remains is the daughter Mime Harrison, Mammy Peggy, and an accumulation of bills. However, Mammy Peggy has kept the "Harrison Pride" alive. She insists on fidelity to the past, and that Mime maintain the posture of "genuine and good quality folk." She does this to such an extent that the marriage of Mime to Bartley, a rich suitor from the North, is endangered. Bartley has come to buy the Harrison plantation. In the process, he falls in love with Mime. Mammy Peggy insists that Mime remember the "Harrison Pride." She demands that the young girl refuse the offer of marriage until it has been made more than once.

Bartley, unaware of this "Southern Pride," refuses to ask for Mime's hand a second time. He accepts her refusal as a definite answer and prepares to return North. When Mime begins to mope and despair, Mammy Peggy hastens to undo what she has done. She informs Bartley of the conditions under which his proposal was rejected. She implores him to try again. On the second try Bartley meets with success. It is clear from the ending of the story that Mammy Peggy will dominate the life of her young mistress and new master as she presumably dominated that of Mime's parents.

"One Man's Fortune" is another story based upon material of which the author had firsthand knowledge. The story deals with aspects of his own life and focuses on the disappointments of a young black man. Although the young man is educated, he still finds that the doors of opportunity are closed to him. At the beginning of the story, three black men, all recent college graduates, sit together planning their futures. They speculate about the nature of the society they are now ready to enter with hopes of earning a living. One of them, Webb Davis, is pessimistic. He has few illusions about America. He questions whether or not they will be able to make a living even though they have their "sheepskins." Charles Mclean is more fortunate than the other two. He has a place waiting for him in his father's "counting room." He is neither optimistic nor pessimistic. Bertram Halliday is optimistic. He believes that the world will grant recognition to him who proves himself worthy. He refuses to believe that a black skin is an obstacle. He believes that there are many men of conscience in the society, and that

these men will look beyond the color of a man's skin and find the real, competent man underneath.

After the meeting, the three men go their separate ways. Halliday returns to his hometown. He intends to continue the study of law. He must first find a job that will allow him to study. He seeks out a white man who showed an interest in him during his high school days. H. G. Featherton, an attorney, is surprised to see him because he had not expected the young man to succeed in college. Halliday asks the attorney for a job and Featherton proceeds to inform the aspirant about the facts of life:

"Well—I should be glad to see you get on, Bert, but as you see, I have nothing in my office that you could do. Now, if you don't mind beginning at the bottom—."

"That's just what I expected to do," Halliday interrupts.

"Why I could speak to the headwaiter of the hotel where I stay. He's a very nice colored man and I have some influence with him. No doubt Charlie could give you a place."

Halliday refuses to believe that a position as a common waiter is all that is open to him. He turns down Mr. Featherton's offer and seeks employment on his own. He makes inquiries at the office of a factory that advertised for clerks, "with preference given to high school boys." He is turned down with an abrupt, "We have nothing for you." Undaunted, he continues to search for work suitable to his education. He discovers that there is none to be found. No one will give him a job as a clerk or salesman. No one will allow him to work in a law office. However, he can find positions as a janitor, and he grudgingly accepts one of these, using his spare time to study law.

After having worked a while as a janitor in a factory, he is approached by Mr. Featherton. The attorney has decided to run "for a seat on the bench" and wants "to ingratiate himself" with the voters in the black section of town. He offers Halliday a job paying five dollars less than he earns at the factory. Halliday accepts because he wants the experience of working in a law office. Because of the young man's hard work in his behalf, Featherton wins the election. One week later, he informs his employee that he must close down the office. Halliday in disappointment leaves. However, "A couple of days later he remembered a book which he had failed to get and returned for it. The office was as usual. Mr. Featherton was a little embarrassed and nervous. At Halliday's desk sat a young white man about his age. He was copying a deed for Mr. Featherton."

Not only is "One Man's Fortune" autobiographical, it also evidences the distance Dunbar had traveled since the optimistic days of *Oak and Ivy*. Like Halliday, he had believed that race was an artificial barrier. He had believed that men could rise above the limitations imposed because of race. Like Booker T. Washington, he had believed that one need only build a better mousetrap than his neighbor, and irrespective of color, the world would beat a path to his door. Yet, because of his skin, severe limitations had been placed upon him. He had been forced into special areas of the literary world just as his people had been forced into special jobs, special neighborhoods, and special associations.

This short story reveals a great deal concerning Dunbar's true sentiments about the racial problem—those that, for the sake of survival, he could not make public. No one who reads "One Man's Fortune" can mistake the voice in the remaining pages of the story for that of anyone but the author. The story should have ended when Halliday walked into his old office to find his position taken over by a white man. Part Four, the section that follows this episode, is unnecessary. Dunbar tacks it on to the main body of the story as if trying to point out something significant to his audience. Nowhere does one find a statement in which Dunbar's pessimism is more explicitly revealed than in Halliday's letter to Davis.

"My dear Webb," the letter reads, "you after all, were right. We have little or no show in the fight for life among these people. I have struggled for two years here at Broughton, and now find myself back where I was when I first stepped out of school with a foolish faith in being equipped for something. One thing, my eyes have been opened anyway, and I no longer judge so harshly the shiftless and unambitious among my people. I hardly see how a people, who have so much to contend with and so little to hope for, can go on striving and aspiring."

Later in the same letter: "They say, too, that our brother Americans sympathize with us, and will help us when we help ourselves. Bah! The only sympathy that I have ever seen on the part of the white man was not for the Negro himself, but for some portion of white blood that the colored man had got tangled up in his veins."

The disappointments, the bitterness, the hostility—all were to be found in *The Strength of Gideon and Other Stories* neatly tucked between the narratives of the plantation tradition. Dunbar did not make an open assault by publicly denouncing the society that continually bent him to its will. But in the face of death, suffering unbearable pain, more and more he began to search for solitude. In those moments, alone with himself, he began to analyze himself objectively and dispassionately and eventually to interpret, in a different light, truths of which he had always been aware.

Dunbar's personal despair was his alone, and he would not share it with his people. They knew what he had to say and were familar with the experiences of the Dunbars and Hallidays of this world. His works had been written for those who did not know. He once believed that if they knew, they would work to change the existing conditions, not for him —for he believed that his journey would soon be over—but for those who would come after him.

For those who would follow, he wrote other things. During one of the many sleepless nights when he could not bear the pain caused by violent coughs wracking his body, he lay in the Colorado night listening to the sound of cattle moving across the plains. Their steps were slow and labored, coming in dull thumps as they trekked to market. He got up from the bed, rushed to his desk, and, despite the pain, began to write:

Slow moves the pageant of a climbing race;
Their footsteps drag far, far below the height,

and the poem, *Slow Through the Dark*, was born.

Looking beyond the present generation to those yet unborn, he continued:

Heed not the darkness round you, dull and deep;
The clouds grow thickest when the summit's nigh,

His message emphasized the necessity for plodding, for holding on despite hardship. He insisted that the path be traveled despite the boulders lying in the way. The poem was written to inspire a race of men; but it was also written as an inspiration to the author whose lamp of hope and faith had burned low indeed.

VIII

THE SPORT OF THE GODS

To have come so near to sing the perfect song
And only by a half-tone lost the key,
There is the potent sorrow, there the grief,
The pale, sad staring of life's tragedy.

In a letter to Attorney Thatcher written in 1902 Dunbar stated: "My plans are few but definite. There is a mid-winter book of poems forthcoming, *Lyrics of Love and Laughter*, and an illustrated one for next fall. An Ohio novel is promised to *Lippincott's*, and dialect stories and verses to various periodicals. Besides this I shall probably read during the latter part of my journey. My appearance is robust but my cough is about as bad as it can be."

After leaving Colorado, Dunbar stopped off in Chicago. He visited his brother and was given a reception in Quinn Chapel. His doctors warned him not to stay too long in Chicago. He had been admonished to leave before the humid weather set in, and so he terminated his visit and returned to Toledo to visit Tobey. They had not met for a year, and, seeing him now, Tobey expressed great concern. He did not tell his fears to Dunbar directly. He didn't have to. The poet was accustomed to the look of apprehension that swept across the faces of strangers when he bent almost double from the force of a cough. It was easy to read such messages in the faces of friends. For a while, they chatted about the early days. Finally, the two absented themselves from their wives and walked off alone, arm in arm—perhaps hoping to find renewed strength in each other.

The poet had become something of a son to this kind, energetic, humanitarian and physician. His concern about the poet's health and disposition, revealed by the sharp, desperate tone that frequently appeared in his voice, was as sincere as that of a father for a son. Dunbar, in turn, looked upon Tobey as a father. Due to the racist nature of America, the physician had been able to perform in this capacity far better than Joshua Dunbar could ever have done. Dunbar remembered how much of his present fame was owed to this man and to other Toledans like him. He knew that Tobey would be worried about him, and this he did not want.

Therefore, he pretended to be happy when he was with Tobey and other friends from the days of *Oak and Ivy*. Even when the pain was most severe, he put forth a smile. His jokes were as witty as ever, and despite the fact that breathing was difficult at times, he even managed a slow dance or two. However, once he was out of Toledo, there was no reason for pretense. He went to Washington to see after the house there and, due to strong pleading from Alice, they again spent the summer in the Catskills.

They returned to Washington in the fall and, despite the lack of change in his condition, Dunbar still continued to give readings. Although his earnings were far from meager, the problem of money continued to plague him. *The Love of Landry* was not well received by the public. However, the collection of short stories, *The Strength of Gideon,* was doing well on the bookstands. In June he received a statement from James Whitcomb Riley informing him that *Lyrics of Lowly Life* had sold over twelve thousand copies—in other words, over a period of six years a volume of poetry had sold at the rate of two thousand per year. This was an almost unprecedented feat for a poet, black or white.

Dunbar had left Colorado in 1900. Twice that year, prior to leaving the West for the last time, he made trips back east. On one of these trips, he had taken his mother to Washington; on another, he had cleared up some business details in the same city. The stay in Colorado had been profitable: It had provided him with material for a novel and a few poems. It had allowed time for solitude and reflection. It had taken him away from the city and thus allowed him to look at its people objectively. Yet it had not returned his strength nor cured his cough. The pains that had previously besieged him were still severe—not only had they not diminished but seemed, if anything, worse than before.

He continued an outward show of pleasantness, yet he was becoming more disgruntled with each passing day. When he was not working at a feverish pace, he was brooding, scolding, or sulking. The private mental pain seemed about to overwhelm him. For the moment the boy in the man had disappeared. The quick mind, capable of evoking "gales of laughter" with the turn of a phrase, of producing humor and humorous verses in an instant, now appeared dulled. Because his doctors had failed to cure him, he sought remedies of his own. One of these, a curious combination which he had stumbled upon by accident, is described by James Weldon Johnson: "I remember how scrupulous I was in seeing that he was provided with the bedtime snack that he wanted every night, a raw onion with salt and a bottle of beer. He had great faith in this smelly combination as an antidote for tuberculosis—the disease that he knew would someday set to naught all antidotes."

Dunbar tried this treatment and many others. None succeeded. Only one thing seemed to bring him partial release: the whiskey which he now began to take in increasingly large doses. He drank regularly before each reading. On one such occasion he drank more than usual, which resulted in an embarrassing incident. The country awoke to the fact that its favorite poet had become an alcoholic.

On October 19th he appeared at a reading in Evanston, Illinois. He had been invited by Professor P. M. Pearson of Northwestern University, and this association with the college meant that the audience was certain to be large. His popularity in the Midwest was exceptionally high, so that not only college students but many residents of the areas were expected to attend. Two days prior to the scheduled reading, while still in Washington, Dunbar had a severe coughing attack. He began to hemorrhage. Again, he resorted to alcohol, which brought temporary relief. The pain was so intense, however, that for days he was forced to walk around like one in a drunken stupor.

He arrived at the recital half an hour late. The audience had already begun to grow impatient. It became apparent as he mounted the platform that something was wrong. He approached the rostrum slowly, as if measuring his steps. He was oblivious to the outstretched hands of the master of ceremonies. He fumbled with his notes. After some time he attempted to read, but the words were jumbled and confused. He hurried over two selections, mumbling the phrases and stumbling over five or six lines. One poem was so poorly rendered that he had to repeat it. The audience grew furious. They began to leave the hall, dragging their children behind them. Dunbar continued to the end, although he cut the program short when he realized what had occurred.

The papers dealt with him as severely on this occasion as they had dealt sympathetically with him during his illness. The feature story in a number of papers told of the poet who was so drunk that he was incapable of giving a coherent reading. No one knew the truth, nor did anyone search for it. The truth was that alcohol was becoming a daily part of Dunbar's nourishment. It was equally true, however, that the intense pressures of his life, work, and illness drove him to seek refuge in the bottle. Nevertheless, despite its negative results, the affair at Evanston had a sobering effect upon him. He postponed readings for a long time, and when he resumed them, he gave them very infrequently. For the most part, he confined himself to the area around Washington, making occasional trips to Florida and New Jersey.

He resumed his heavy work load. To the poems and short stories he added essays, which were reflections on the social life of black people in Washington. In January he had written an article entitled, "Negro Life in Washington." He extended this article, retitled it "Negro Society in Washington," and published it in the *Saturday Evening Post*. He completed a third novel, *The Fanatics* and an illustrated volume of poetry, *Candle Lightin' Time*. In his leisure time, of which there was little, he entertained friends in his Spruce Street home and continued to war against his illness.

The Fanatics was published in 1901, and the reception it received was disappointing. He had spent countless painful and sleepless nights laboring over the plot of the story. He had crossed out phrases, torn up whole pages, and rewritten entire sections. He wanted the novel to stand as a monument to his contribution to literature. He had chosen his theme well. The sectional strife of the Civil War—when a nation was internally torn, when the conflict of loyalties between North and South were often reflected in private households, affecting the relationships between son and father, brother and brother—was not far from the memory of the reading public of 1901. It had been a time of turmoil.

Yet from the turmoil was to come a lasting peace. A nation would be solidified; two warring camps would be turned into one country; North and South would labor under the same flag for the common good of a united nation.

The turmoil drew Dunbar's interest as a writer. Nations, he knew, sometimes acted like individuals. Every man, like every nation, had two sides to his personality. One side was often chaotic, sometimes causing quarrels and war; the other sought peace and stability. Sometimes the warring side was dominant, and then man and nation alike were thrown into turmoil. However, the other side continued to search for peace, continued to attempt to unify the whole.

Such a struggle was taking place within Dunbar. He was a young man—only twenty-nine—yet he had grown old before his time. His face never lost its youthful, boyish appearance, yet his slow-moving body gave evidence of the wear and tear that comes only with age. Like the nation, he had experienced internal warfare, and the events of the past year had made each day appear to be filled with discord. He had dreamed of finding peace in Colorado, though not by confronting his problems but by running from them. Yet, perhaps he had been wrong. To return to nature, to the land, might not be enough to unite the warring factions inside him. Perhaps he would have to meet them openly, face up to them, and search for a lasting peace through direct confrontation.

As he had done before in *The Uncalled* and in *The Love of Landry*, he sought to work out his personal problem through the medium of fiction. The theme, peculiar to his other novels, runs through this one also: the constant demand for freedom, the assertion that man must be released from all restrictions. The image of the bird in the cage was still real in his mind; and as he had imagined the bird to be bruising and bloodying its wings in an attempt to gain freedom, so too did he imagine the same for his character and his nation.

Again, the major characters of his novel are white, and it is with them that he identifies. However, a novel centered around the Civil War must deal with the black man's part in it. Therefore, for the first time, black characters receive a role in a Dunbar novel, though a subordinate one. Nigger Ed, the town crier, is one such character, and of all the failures of the book, Nigger Ed fails the most. The poet attempted to portray a man who underwent experiences of the kind that even the author did not believe possible. Nigger Ed was to be treated as a man transformed from the town buffoon into a man accepted by his community after participation in the Civil War.

Early in the novel the author tells us that "Nigger Ed has a picturesque knack for lying." In addition, the town crier is also the town drunk. He provides amusement for the town until war comes, when he marches off at the side of the town's men. When he returns, Dunbar speaks of the transformation of the town and its new-found respect for Ed: "There were women who begged him to come in and talk to them about their sons who had been left on some Southern field, wives who wanted to hear over again the last words of their loved ones. And so they gave him a place for life and everything he wanted. . . ." After relating the experiences of Bertram Halliday in the short story, "One Man's Fortune," Dunbar could not possibly have *believed* in such a conversion as that which he attributes to the town.

The major characters of the novel represent North and South. The larger conflict in the nation is mirrored by the conflict within themselves. Bradford Waters is a Union supporter; Stephen Van Doren, a supporter of the Confederacy. The town is affected by the conflict, its citizens divided in sympathy between Unionists and Confederates. The conflict affects the engagement between Robert, the son of Van Doren, and Mary, the daughter of Waters. When Robert joins the southern forces, Mary's father insists that his daughter break the engagement. Rebelling against her father, she refuses, and the author relates: "She loved Bob, not his politics. What had she to do with those black men down there in the South, it was none of her business."

Others in the town felt the same way. Another conflict is nearly averted when escaping blacks attempt to settle in the town of Dorsbury. The threat of blacks settling among the citizens of the town divides the town into factions just as the war had done. "For the time all party lines fell away, and all the people were united in one cause—resistance of the black horde." At the close of the novel, the Van Dorens and the Waterses are reconciled. Their period of fanaticism, like that of the nation, is over, and they will live together in union.

The Fanatics is a bad novel; it is far worse than *The Love of Landry*. The reason is that Dunbar was attempting to reconcile too many disparate elements. He wanted to reconcile North and South, Waters and Van Doren, Robert and Mary. In addition, he wanted to reconcile Nigger Ed with the town and, through Ed, the black men who sought refuge in the town. The result is that the attempt at reconciliation fails. For all of Dunbar's attempts to portray Nigger Ed as a changed character, he remains a buffoon at the end of the novel. More important, however, there is no reconciliation between the escaped slaves and the town. They are the most alienated group in *The Fanatics*. Unwanted by the North, mistreated by the South, they are men without a country. Whatever union may eventually come about as the result of peace between the two warring factions of the nation, there will be no union with the new freedom except on the terms that prevailed during slavery.

Dunbar sought to examine the conflict within himself and impose it upon his novel; yet, he was far from pleased with his labors. Like the escaped slaves, he also remained a man without a home. The one that had been offered to him would be granted only on terms which he could not wholly accept. In his own mind the side of his personality that called out for peace and that which called out for rebellion could not exist with one another. Even as he pictured Nigger Ed arriving at the point of universal acceptance, he felt universal rejection in his own heart.

He was forced to conclude that the world belonged not to the Nigger Eds or the escaped slaves, but instead to the Van Dorens and the Waterses. The blacks had places in it, but these places were selected and defined by others. The nation that had made Nigger Ed a buffoon was unlikely to raise him to the status of human being. The nation that had fooled itself into believing it had fought a war to free the slaves, was not likely to extend its generosity further.

The Fanatics was one of Dunbar's most fervent pleas in prose for compassion and understanding. It was his most eloquent appeal for peace. As a failure, therefore, the novel ranks among his most pessimistic. In failing to reconcile the conflicting forces in the novel, he failed also to reconcile those within himself. Standing in the shadow of death, he had hoped for some saving grace, some acknowledgment of a mutual respect between the world and himself. Having journeyed back from suicidal despair in Colorado, he had sought peace—a serenity, which did not involve a journey from man, but rather one which led to man.

No such peace was possible. The world in which he lived out his last years was a fast changing one, and the statement he put into the mouth of Nanette, one of his characters in *The Fanatics*, is an apt summary of the state of affairs at the turn of the century: "Everyone is mad, you and I and all of us. When shall we come to our senses?" To this, a beleaguered Dunbar could only have replied—Never!

He was caught up in a world wherein new and powerful forces were at play, which in his despair, he was unable to understand. He turned to the bottle more frequently now in an attempt to drown out not only his pain, but his sorrow as well. His home remained the center of Washington life. Guests from all over the country continued to pay their respects. Yet he knew that they were paying their respects to a ghost, to a hollow man, one whose strength had been dissipated by a lifetime of inner conflict. Nevermind that the country continued to honor him; nevermind that President McKinley sent a special envoy to ask him to participate in the inaugural parade. Nevermind that more and more requests for poetry, short stories, and articles poured in upon him. The turn of the century found him ill equipped to deal with the future and unable to meet the rigid requirements of living as a black man and black artist in a world so different from that of the previous century.

The nineteenth century had been a century of compromise. Men attempted to bring opposing elements together and forge them into one workable unit. In this spirit, Dunbar was a natural. Having sought compromise all of his life, he was almost one with an age in which compromise was the norm. However, the country was not prepared for the price of compromise in the area of race relations. The resurgence of the Ku Klux Klan and other white vigilante groups, the intimidation of blacks at the polls, the race conflagration

—North and South—all militated against reconciliation between black and white.

The society declared total war on its black population, and a response in kind was due from the "acknowledged leader" of the race. Booker T. Washington, the most articulate spokesman before the close of the century, had, like Dunbar, been incapable of confronting the challenge of the twentieth century. He would live until 1915, but the policies of peace and reconciliation that he fostered had died long before. Dunbar could have taken up his pen and plunged into this war with the same vigor he displayed in attempts at reconciliation. However, only in a few instances did he stir himself to battle.

Once, while entertaining a visitor in his Washington home, he was told of a lynching at which the visitor had been a spectator. After watching the man intensely throughout the conversation, seeing his face turn from bewilderment to grotesque horror as he relived the scene he had witnessed, Dunbar was impatient to put the story on paper. The man had hardly left the front steps before he dashed to his room and began writing *The Haunted Oak*, a poem in which the story of the lynching is told by the tree upon which the act took place.

The tree relates the tale to a passerby, who stops to inquire about its bareness. The events which led up to the lynching are graphically revealed. The prisoner was caught and charged "with the old, old crime" and remanded to jail. Later he was taken from the jail by a group of vigilantes who managed to "[fool] the jailer with lying words." The group contains some of the most respected men in the community—the minister, the judge, and the doctor. With these distinguished men looking on with the others, the prisoner is hung from the tree. Because of this act the limbs of the oak

tree are destined to remain bare, for no sap will ever return to its boughs. In the thirteenth stanza, the oak utters
the words that might well have been uttered by the author
himself:

> *I feel the rope against my bark,*
> *And the weight of him in my grain,*
> *I feel in the throe of his final woe*
> *The touch of my own last pain.*

Further than this, Dunbar would not go. His own pain
stood in his way. He might sympathize with the hanged
man and lash out in anger at those who bore the deaths of
such men on their consciences, but he would not initiate a
sustained, all-out protest against the forces that made reconciliation impossible on a national level. The twentieth
century demanded total warfare against racism not an accommodation with it; and to wage total warfare, one had to
be capable of quieting the tumult within his own breast.
This Dunbar could not do. The best he could manage was
the peace he had effected between his hero and heroine in
The Fanatics. This, however, was an artificial peace, not a
lasting one—either for him or the nation.

Shortly after the turn of the century, both the poet and
the nation were stunned into awareness: the accommodation
made by each had brought not peace, but chaos. The blow
suffered by Dunbar was heavier than that suffered by the
nation. His marriage, begun when one poet read the works
of another, came to an end in 1902. One can only speculate
about the causes. Dunbar's inability to come to grips with
his own private desperation almost assuredly contributed
to the breakup. He had changed a great deal since Colorado.
The child of nature was now the man of desperation. The

man whom Alice pictured as being capable of bringing back the true meaning of violets to her life, had proved incapable of putting together the pieces of his own. The war he carried within himself, having intensified over the years, entered his married life as well. The alcohol he used to combat pain, was now used to combat other problems as well. Gone was the poet of yesterday, the man who had sought a non-existent beauty, who had refused to believe that the world could not be reformed, that a public which had grown to love him as a singer of songs would not, in due time, accept the message of any song he sang.

James Weldon Johnson, who knew him throughout his career, has written: "As a man, Dunbar was kind and tender. In conversation he was brilliant and polished. . . . In his actions he was as impulsive as a child, sometimes even erratic, indeed, his intimate friends almost looked upon him as a spoiled child."

Later, Johnson gave this assessment: "He was the Dunbar of the courtly manners, polished speech, and modest behavior . . . but as lovable as he was with people he liked, I learned that under his tongue there was a sac of bitter sarcasm that he spat out on people he did not like, and often used in his own defense."

Sarcasm became his chief means of defense. The poet gave way under pressure and became the spoiled child who believed himself beset by enemies. Soon those who were closest to him became the objects of his scorn. He loved his wife. He would be saddened by her departure. And Alice loved him! In the years to come she would write of him with a compassion and a tenderness that no biographer could ever approach. Yet Dunbar's personal problems were so deeply ingrained, his bitterness so well hidden, and the censure he leveled against himself so strong, that the twentieth century brought his marriage tumbling down upon his head.

The marriage built by the nation was also coming apart. The rupture occurred in 1903, one year after the breakup of Dunbar's marriage. The union between the races wrought by that astute minister, Booker T. Washington, was endangered. The black partners of that marriage, had turned their ears to strange, seductive whisperings. They were listening to a brash, Harvard-educated scholar from Massachusetts, W. E. Burghardt Du Bois.

When Du Bois published *The Souls of Black Folk* in 1903, he set high standards for the black writer—standards that only those of conviction and courage could meet. Like Dunbar, he had undergone intensive soul searching, he had been engaged in constant conflict with his own nature. Unlike Dunbar, however, Du Bois emerged from his period of despondency a new man—one who had united the fierce elements within his own being to declare total war upon a society in which injustice flourished unchecked.

Du Bois was born in Great Barrington, Massachusetts, in 1868, three years after the Civil War. He traced his parentage back to the French Huguenots. Early in life he discovered that he was not like the other children of Great Barrington, that "a veil" seemed to separate him from them. But despite racial difficulties encountered in high school, he finished at the top of his class, graduated with honors and entered Fisk University in Nashville, Tennessee. This was the first of three universities which he would attend, finally receiving a Doctor of Philosophy degree from Harvard University.

At Fisk, Du Bois discovered the oneness of purpose between himself and his people, which would lead to his later work. Unlike Dunbar, he did not attempt to interpret the lives of his people without firsthand knowledge of his subject. He had been born in a city with a predominately white population and educated in an otherwise all-white school; yet he refused to accept the definition offered him concerning a people with whom he had established only a spiritual relationship. He found out at Fisk, and later at Atlanta, that blacks were held down not because of their own inadequacies, but because a system dedicated to racism would not permit them to progress. He came to teach and in the end learned far more than he taught.

He learned that the evil confronting blacks had been born of a tradition that had roots outside the South, even beyond the shores of America. These roots reached all the way back to the old world. The problem was as old as man himself; yet Du Bois believed that it was more threatening here in the twentieth century than at any previous time. It was "the problem of the color line," a line which divided one man from another and which, in too many instances, made one man subject to the tyranny of another. Therefore, he stated, not once but many times, "the problem of the twentieth century is the problem of the color line."

A man's commitment was to be measured according to the energy he spent in attempting to erase this line. Those who ignored this challenge gave sanction to the legitimacy of caste barriers through inaction. Du Bois held these men in the deepest contempt. This meant that, inevitably, there would be a confrontation with Booker T. Washington. After careful soul searching, Du Bois published *The Souls of Black Folk*, which brought the confrontation to public attention.

He was not the only black man to contest the Washington

program. Many believed that the Washington solution was a sellout to the white South. Even Dunbar disagreed with the educator on certain fundamental parts of his program—he did not accept Washington's educational formula—yet he remained on good terms with Washington. Monroe Trotter, the gifted editor of the Boston *Guardian,* and a Harvard graduate like Du Bois, disliked every aspect of Washington's program and showed his dislike in serious personal attacks on Washington.

Du Bois' objections were those of the scholar. He carefully thought through the pros and cons of what was being offered. His overall opposition is summed up in the following statement: "Mr. Washington represents in Negro thought the old attitude of adjustment and submission." To Du Bois, adjustment meant that one accepted the world as it was, that one believed the condition of the black man to be static, his life ordained by blind fate. This was in line with Dunbar's beliefs. Submission meant to accept injustice, disfranchisement, and discrimination as the penalties imposed upon inferiors whose position warranted them little more.

The Souls of Black Folk is a repudiation of the Washington program. But it is much more: it is a message addressed to black people in the lyrical, flowing words of a poet; a message that lays waste the myths and fantasies of the past. Men might still cling to their belief in "the minstrel Negro," in the Negro of the plantation school of literature. However, after Du Bois it was impossible to accept such characters rationally without bringing one's own sanity into question.

What black people had wanted from their poets they received from one who called himself not a poet, but a scholar and a sociologist. It was as a poet, however, that he endeared himself to his people; and it was as a poet that he mounted the attack against racism and oppression. For no other man since David Walker in the nineteenth century, could it be said more truthfully that words were weapons. He used them to attack a society that victimized men because of color; yet he also used them as weapons against ignorance. No poet was more concerned than he about bringing a sense of self-awareness to his people, and none did more in this respect.

"Of Our Spiritual Strivings," the opening essay in *The Souls of Black Folk,* is a call for awareness based upon Du Bois' personal problems with his identity. History and tradition had sought to impose definitions on him; they had labeled him and placed him in accordance with their ideas of his capabilities. The compulsion to believe myths about oneself, to accept what a powerful nation dictates as truth, is almost irresistible. Therefore, wrote Du Bois, "the Negro is a sort of seventh son, born with a veil, and gifted with second sight in this American world—a world which yields him no true self-consciousness, but only lets him see himself through the revelation of the other world. It is a peculiar sensation, this double-consciousness, this sense of always looking at one's self through the eyes of others, of measuring one's soul by the tape of a world that looks on in amused contempt and pity. One never feels his twoness—an American, a Negro, two souls, two thoughts, two unreconciled strivings; two warring ideals in one dark body, whose dogged strength alone keeps it from being torn asunder."

Who am I? Du Bois asked himself out of despair and concluded, I am a black man who would not "Africanize America, for America has too much to teach the world and Africa." I am a black man, who will not "bleach his Negro soul in a flood of white Americanism, for he knows that Negro blood has a message for the world." I am a black man who "simply wishes to make it possible for a man to be both a Negro and an American, . . . without having the doors of Opportunity closed roughly in his face."

To those who answered him with contempt, who reminded him of his "place," who claimed that he was a ward in their country, he answered: "Your country? How came it yours? Before the Pilgrims landed we were here. Here we have brought our three gifts and mingled them with yours: a gift of story and song—soft, stirring melody in an ill-harmonized and unmelodious land, the gift of sweat and brawn to beat back the wilderness, conquer the soil, and lay the foundations of this vast economic empire two hundred years earlier than your weak hands could have done it; the third, a gift of the Spirit. . . . Our song, our toil, our cheer, and warning have been given to this nation in blood-brotherhood. Are not these gifts worth giving? Is not this work and striving? Would America have been America without her Negro people?" Black people had found a new champion and a new poet.

Dunbar left Washington soon after his separation from his wife. This city where there were so many friends and so many memories, reminded him of what few pleasures there had been in his later life. He went back to Dayton, back to the town from which he had come five years before, then hardly more than a boy. As usual, he worked frantically, as if each poem or story might be his last. The house in Dayton soon began to hum with the noise and laughter of visitors who came from all over the country to see him. He was, as usual, the well-mannered host, although he began to leave his guests sooner and more frequently with each visit. His pain continued and so too did his drinking.

In 1902 he published what was to be his last novel. *The Sport of the Gods* is a product of the years of illness. It was written during the period when the pain was most severe, when the hemorrhaging was most constant, and when the cough was most wracking. In a conversation with a friend, he spoke of the time during which he wrote this novel. "When I first began my career, I wrote rapidly, accomplishing without difficulty five thousand words a day. Now I write slowly—oh! so slowly. I sometimes spend three weeks on a chapter and then am not satisfied with the result. . . . Last spring, when filling an order for a prose composition for *Lippincott's* magazine, I wrote fifty thousand words in thirty days, but I have never recovered from the strain of it."

The Sport of the Gods marked a new turn for Dunbar in many ways. For the first time he dealt with blacks as major figures in a novel; he made the environment which produced crime and degeneracy the novel's chief villain. In no other novel does the city come under as fierce an attack from Dunbar's pen. The city is portrayed as the center of evil, vice, sin, and corruption. Into this hellhole falls the family of Berry Hamilton, a victim of the southern plantation system, whose daughter and son are ruined by this hostile environment.

Berry Hamilton, hardworking, thrifty butler on the plantation of Maurice Oakley, is falsely accused of having stolen money from his employer's half brother, Francis. Although the money was stolen by Francis himself, Berry is convicted of the crime and sentenced to two years in jail. Because of the hostility of the community, Berry's family—his wife Fannie, daughter Kit, and son Joe—move to New York City. In Harlem, the young Hamiltons undergo a change. Joe becomes a pimp and later a murderer. Kit becomes a dancer. After being told that her marriage to Berry is illegal, Fannie marries a drifter who treats her cruelly. Upon being released from prison, Berry makes his way to New York, finds that his family has been torn apart, and manages to become reunited with his wife after her second husband dies.

The novel ends on a happy note. Upon hearing the story of Berry's frameup, a one-time newspaper man goes South to investigate. Due to his persistence, Francis confesses, Maurice goes mad, and Berry, his good name restored, returns to the South with his wife.

Dunbar evidences his intention to move away from the plantation tradition in the first paragraph of the novel. "Fiction," he writes, "has said so much in regret of the old days when there were plantations and overseers and masters and slaves that it was good to come upon such a household as Berry Hamilton's, if for no other reason than that it afforded a relief from the monotony of tiresome literation."

Nevertheless, the theme of the plantation tradition remains central to the novel. As Berry heads for home with his wife, the reader is led to believe that the corruption that destroyed his family in the North is non-existent in the South. Yet, it was in the South that the initial crime, which forced the Hamilton family North, occurred. Moreover, Berry differs little from hundreds of plantation slaves and workers who, hardworking and faithful, pledge allegiance to their masters. Only the old southern master is different from Dunbar's earlier fiction. Maurice is not the kind master of antebellum days, but the harsh vindictive master who has been pointed out in countless slave narratives. At last Dunbar admits that the loyalty exhibited by the slave was not returned in kind by the master.

The emphasis upon the city as a place of corruption is not new to Dunbar's fiction. In the short stories, "The Truthfulness of Polly" and "Jimsella," he had already dealt with the evil influences of the city on his characters. Part of this animosity toward the city stemmed from his romance with nature, from a belief that the country life was far superior to that of the city. What is important in this book is that the emphasis on destiny is more pronounced here than in his other books; it is as though the poet had irrevocably resigned himself to "cruel fate."

The lines that he used to close the novel on the life of the Hamilton family might well have served as the prelude to the closing of the book on his life: "It was not a happy life, but it was all that was left to them, and they took it up without complaint, for they knew they were powerless against some will infinitely stronger than their own." So too was the author. He was now convinced of this, and as he awaited that death which he was certain would soon come, he arrived at the conclusion that man was little more than a puppet pulled along by strings—held aloft by forces which he himself could not define or combat.

That such was the culmination of his thinking is perhaps the greatest sadness of his long years of sorrow. The boy who had begun with the idea of conquering the world, of carving out a place for himself with the power of his own creative imagination, now resigned himself to a fate over which he had no control. True to the ethic of the nineteenth century, he had believed in the theory of the survival of the fittest; he believed that the world of man would always open a path for those who proved themselves to be among the fittest. When one is forced to forsake such ideals, perhaps, as the poet John Keats has written, ". . . it seems best to die."

IX

BENEATH THE WILLOWS IN THE GRASS

Because I had loved so deeply,
Because I had loved so long,
God in His great compassion
Gave me the gift of song.

On December 30, 1905, Dunbar informed a visitor: "I am lying fallow. I believe my soul has become greatly impoverished, and it will take a good many rains and snows to put anything into it worth coming out in blossom. But my greatest help will be the knowledge that my friends keep in touch with me, and now and then a line like an electric spark flashes from one to the other and I am new again." He would never be new again, and he knew it. For almost two years he had been an invalid. Most of the day and night he was confined to bed. Visitors often found him propped up on a sofa—in later days, he would be found in bed—dictating to a stenographer. The illness had worn down his body. Yet miraculously, for the first time in his life, he appeared calm. He was more at peace with himself during these times than at any previous time. Visitors frequently commented on his cheerful disposition.

Mary Church Terrell was one such visitor. A black woman whose fight for social and racial justice is well known, she had been a neighbor of the Dunbars in Washington. When she was in Dayton to address a meeting of the Ohio Federation of Colored Women's Clubs, Mrs. Terrell visited her former neighbor. She found him sitting in a chair under the watchful eyes of his mother. "Sometimes," she remarked, "I am tempted to believe you are just playing the role of interested invalid, so as to receive the sympathy and the homage of these beautiful girls."

His face lit up. A smile came to his eyes. He threw back his head and laughed. "Sometimes I think I am just loafing, myself," he replied. He could never forget the joke, nor the meaning intended. The pleasantry was kind, and in those days he appreciated the kindness of old friends. The spoiled boy of whom James Weldon Johnson had written had now disappeared. In his place was a young man with lines in his face suggesting a maturity beyond his years. He hemorrhaged constantly, almost every day and, although drugs brought temporary relief from the cough, this was only temporary, and he never knew at what time his body would be violently assaulted again.

As far as possible, he managed to be cheerful with his guests. Great men and men not so great, statesmen and poets, rich men and poor men—all came to pay homage to him. With each he shared a cup of tea, a laugh, and a memory. One visitor, Doctor Robert Burns, was a constant companion. The two had grown up together in Dayton and pursued separate professions; yet each had reserved a space in his heart for the other. Visiting him almost daily, Burns served in the capacity of friend and physician. Dunbar needed both in those final months.

The dawn of the new century brought with it acts of repression almost unequaled in American history. It was as if the nation—North, East, South, and West—had gone mad. One hundred black men and women were lynched in the first year of the new century. These lynchings took place in all areas of the country. The most spectacular incident occurred in August of 1904. Two black men were accused of murdering a white farmer and his family. They were jailed in Statesboro, Georgia, and later transferred to Savannah for "safe keeping." When they were brought back to Statesboro to stand trial, they were convicted and given the death sentence.

The white citizens, however, could not wait. Burning with a fierce hatred for all things black, they attacked black men, women, and children in the streets, in their homes, and wherever they were to be found. Blacks stayed off of the streets. They refused to go to work or to leave their homes for food. On the day of the sentencing, a white mob broke into the courtroom, seized the two men from a company of state militia "whose rifles were not loaded in tender consideration for the feelings of the mob." The blacks were taken out and burned alive. In the aftermath, a black woman and her infant son were beaten and kicked, and her husband murdered. Not even the locked doors of the houses of the black population saved them from the wrath of Statesboro's enraged citizenry. Homes were wrecked and burned and their occupants were beaten. Thousands of blacks were forced to leave the town.

Nor was the North spared its share of the national madness. In Springfield, Ohio, not far from Dayton where Dunbar lay ill, a race riot occurred in the year of 1904. A white officer was shot by a black man during a scuffle. The black was captured and placed in jail. A white mob broke into the prison, shot the prisoner in the doorway of his cell, hung his body to a telegraph pole, and proceeded, like madmen, to empty their guns into the limp, dead body. The orgy of violence continued on into the black section of town where the Ohio night reeked with the smoke from burning homes, rang with the screams of beaten men, women, and children, and was pierced by the bestial howls of a white mob composed of men from every segment of the community.

As these events were taking place, the influence of Dunbar's old friend Booker T. Washington was beginning to wane among black people. The reasoned, scholarly assault on his policies by the young Dr. Du Bois had precipitated more attacks. Dunbar's friend and Washington neighbor, Kelly Miller, a professor at Howard University, had finally swung over to the opposition, swelling the ranks of the black intellectuals who opposed Washington's policies. In July of 1905 and again in 1906, a group of intellectuals, under the leadership of Dr. Du Bois, met at Niagara Falls, Canada. They drew up a manifesto that summed up the events of the early years of the new century and revealed the new fighting mood of the Afro-Americans.

The resolution stated in part: "In the past year the work of the Negro hater has flourished in the land. Step by step the defenders of the rights of American citizens have retreated. The work of stealing the black man's ballot has progressed and the fifty and more representatives of stolen votes still sit in the nation's capital. . . . Never before in the modern age has a great and civilized folk threatened to adopt so cowardly a creed in the treatment of its fellow citizens, born and bred on its soil. Stripped of verbiage and subterfuge and in its naked nastiness, the new American creed says: Fear to let black men even try to rise lest they become the equals of the white. And this in the land that professes to follow Jesus Christ. The blasphemy of such a course is only matched by its cowardice."

Dunbar could not have been oblivious to these events. He knew, however, that he could take no part in them. That he was saddened is beyond doubt. He had always wished for racial peace just as he had wished for peace within himself. There had never been racial peace, either in his lifetime or anyone else's. In the nineteenth century it had been possible to believe in the illusion. This was so no longer. This was the age of the realist, in letters as well as life, and the time of the dreamer had passed. Within Dunbar, however, there remained elements of both the realist and the dreamer. The realist in him cried out in bitterness—in despair—as evidenced in this poem to Frederick Douglass:

> *Ah, Douglass, we have fall'n on evil days,*
> > *Such days as thou, not even thou didst know,*
> > *When thee, the eyes of that harsh long ago*
> *Saw, salient, at the cross of devious ways,*
> *And all the country heard thee with amaze.*
> > *Not ended then, the passionate ebb and flow,*
> > *The awful tide that battled to and fro;*
> *We ride amid a tempest of dispraise.*
>
> *Now, when the waves of swift dissension swarm,*
> > *And Honor, the strong pilot, lieth stark,*
> *Oh, for thy voice high-sounding o'er the storm,*
> > *For thy strong arm to guide the shivering bark,*
> *The blast-defying power of thy form,*
> > *To give us comfort through the lonely dark.*

The dreamer cried out in hopeful if not optimistic tones: "Heart of the Southland, heed me pleading now," he began the poem, *To the South*, which he subtitled "On Its New Slavery." The poem is a plea. The poet enumerates the long list of deeds warranting better treatment for black men and women:

> *Whose infancy our mother's hands have nursed.*
> *Thy manhood, gone to battle unaccursed,*
> *Our fathers left to till th' reluctant field,*
> *To rape the soil for what she would not yield;*

And later:

> *Too long the rumors of thy hatred go*
> *For those who loved thee and thy children so.*

After such words of despair concerning lost love, he goes on to scale the heights of sentimentality. In lines that Du Bois would certainly have called whining and loathesome, Dunbar calls the South's attention to the former loyal servant in stanzas that rank among the most disgusting in black poetry:

> *Now all is changed, within the rude stockade*
> *A bondsman whom the greed of men has made*
> *Almost too brutish to deplore his plight,*
> *Toils hopeless on from joyous morn till night.*

> *For him no more the cabin's quiet rest,*
> *The homely joys that gave to labor zest;*
> *No more for him the merry banjo's sound,*
> *Nor trip of lightsome dances footing round.*

The contradictions between these two poems are magnified in the volume *Lyrics of Love and Laughter*. Published in 1903, this book appeared four years after *Lyrics of the Hearthside*. In it are included the poems of the years of depression and tension, of the sojourn in Colorado, of the search for health, of the breakup of his marriage. For the first time in a book of poetry, his dialect poems are almost as numerous as those in pure English. Unlike the poems in *Lyrics of the Hearthside*, they are intermingled. One finds, therefore, such poems as *The Poet*, Dunbar's most important statement on dialect poetry and the one that evidences his opposition to the writing of it, sandwiched in between two poems written in dialect, *In the Morning* and *Li'l Gal*. The bitterness and despondency illustrated in *Douglass*, by the lament that the hero is no longer present to lead the race, is obscured by the tribute to Booker T. Washington: "A peer of princes in the world acclaim,/Master spirit for the Nations needs/Strong, silent, purposeful beyond his kind."

The servile description of black men in *To the South*, is offset by *Black Samson of Brandywine*, which tells the tale of Samson, a black hero who died in the battle of Brandywine:

> *Was he a freeman or bondman?*
> *Was he a man or a thing?*
> *What does it matter? His brav'ry*
> *Renders him royal—a king.*
> *If he was only a chattel,*
> *Honor the ransom may pay*
> *Of the royal, the loyal black giant*
> *Who fought for his country that day.*

The poem *The Unsung Heroes* pays further tribute to men who certainly did not long for "the cabin's quiet rest":

A song for the unsung heroes who stood the awful test,
When the humblest host that the land could boast went forth to meet the best;

A song for the unsung heroes who fell on the bloody sod,
Who fought their way from night to day and struggled up
to God.

The most striking contradiction of all is that between *To the*
South and *The Haunted Oak*. *The Haunted Oak* paints a
portrait of the South which no words can erase.

Despite serious shortcomings in selection, there were
poems in *Lyrics of Love and Laughter* that rank among
those in previous volumes. One of the most important is
Life's Tragedy. Here the poet weaves the twin tragedies of
his life into a poetical pattern. Since the age of six when he
first began to put words on paper in stanzaic form, his dream
had been that of every poet: to sing the perfect song, to
write a poem so complete in meter, rhythm, and message
that it would stand forever as a well-wrought work of art.
And when he had stumbled upon the picture of the plain
but pretty face with the deep, sensitive, thoughtful eyes, he
had dreamed the dream of every lover—to find the perfect
partner with whom to share the perfect love.

Life's Tragedy laments his inability to attain these goals.
Yet, he is despondent not because they were unattained, but
because he had come so close to attaining them:

> *This, this it is to be accursed indeed;*
> *For if we mortals love, or if we sing,*
> *We count our joys not by the things we have,*
> *But by what kept us from the perfect thing.*

Lyrics of Love and Laughter was not his last book. An
illustrated volume of poems, *Howdy, Honey, Howdy,* and
Lyrics of Sunshine and Shadow followed. However, neither
measured up to its predecessors, and with the exception of

A Lost Dream included in *Lyrics of Sunshine and Shadow,* few of the new poems are distinctive. The same can be said about his later prose. Two volumes of short stories, *In Old Plantation Days* and *The Heart of Happy Hollow* add nothing to his reputation as a writer of prose. He had written his best fictional work, *The Sport of the Gods,* years earlier, and neither of the works that followed could equal this.

In November of 1905, Doctor Robert Burns, his lifelong friend and companion, died after a short and sudden illness. Dunbar, who had for so long been faced with the prospect of death himself, found it difficult to believe that another had suffered the fate meant for him. Against the objections of his physicians, he left his sick bed to pay his final respects to this long-time friend. However, even after the funeral, he could never bring himself to believe that "Bud" was gone. Now his life became one of quiet waiting. In a letter to a friend, he explained what this meant: "My life consists of going to bed at the beginning of the month and staying there, with very brief intervals of half an hour or so, until the beginning of the month. . . . Of course there are some friends who come in, and some books that I occasionally get to read, but usually I am studying the pattern of the ceiling until I could make a very clever sketch of it from memory without the trouble of learning to draw."

Soon the long vigil with death began in earnest. The countdown proceeded slowly. After the Christmas holidays, he took a turn for the worse. Not only was he hemorrhaging more, but he experienced difficulties with breathing that he had never encountered before. Throughout the first month of the new year, he lay in critical condition. With few exceptions, visitors were barred from his bedside. He was attended by his mother whose long, sleepless nights were a gauge of the steady deterioration of his condition.

By the second week of February, there was no doubt that the end was in sight. He became delirious, inquiring repeatedly about time—about the hour of the day and the day of the week. On February 9th a physician was hastily called. After a few hours, a minister was also summoned. On arriving at the bedside, the minister began to recite the Twenty-Third Psalm. From somewhere within, Dunbar searched for the strength to repeat after the minister. The words came haltingly from his lips. He managed to repeat one line; then he slowly closed his eyes, opened them again for a short time, murmured some inaudible phrase, and closed his eyes—this time forever.

On February 12th the friends and survivors of Paul Laurence Dunbar gathered at the Baker Street African Methodist Episcopal Church, to pay tribute to his memory. Doctor Tobey was almost as distraught as the poet's mother. When called upon to speak, he found it difficult to produce words through a steady flow of tears. After several attempts, he finally composed himself and read a letter from Toledo's Mayor, Brand Whitlock, whose words summed up the agony and suffering that had led to the poet's death as no formal eulogy could. Whitlock wrote: "I know something of his deeper sufferings, something of the disease that really killed him. I can never forget the things he said about this that last evening we spent together. That last evening he recited his *Ships That Pass in the Night*. . . . I sat and listened, conscious that I would not hear him again, knowing that voice would soon be mute. I can hear him now and see the expression on his fine face as he said Passing! Passing! It was prophetic."

His final resting place was the Woodlawn cemetery in Dayton. He was buried near a large oak tree. Three years later, on his birthday, a monument was erected on the spot by the citizens of Dayton in an attempt to pay tribute to his memory. Inscribed on the bronze plate were the lines:

"Lay me down beneaf de willers in de grass,
Whah de branch'll go a-singin' as it pass.
An' w'en I's a-layin' low,
I kin hyeah it as it go
Singin', 'Sleep, ma honey, tek yo' res' at las'."

From the pen of an old friend came what was, perhaps the most perfect epitaph of all: "God keep his gentle soul and may he find in that world where the spirits of just men are made perfect—that rest which on earth he never knew."

CHRONOLOGY

1872   Born on June 27, in Dayton, Ohio.

1891   Graduated from Central High School, with honors. Composed school song. Obtained job as elevator operator in Callahan Building.

1892   Became member of Western Association of Writers, in Dayton.
Completed *Oak and Ivy*.

1893   Met Charles Thatcher, an attorney from Toledo, Ohio, who became influential in helping Dunbar launch his career as a poet.
Worked at Chicago World's Fair. There met Frederick Douglass.

1895   Completed *Majors and Minors*.
Began what would become life-long friendship with Dr. H. A. Tobey, superintendent of the State Hospital for the Insane in Toledo. He, too, would be influential in launching Dunbar's career.

1896   *Lyrics of Lowly Life*. Review of this book by critic William Dean Howells establishes Dunbar's reputation as a poet on national level.

1897   Toured England. Became assistant in Library of Congress, where he remained until December of 1898. Composed "Tuskegee Song" for Booker T. Washington's Tuskegee Institute.

1898   Married Alice Ruth Moore of New Orleans.
The Uncalled, a novel; *Folks from Dixie*, collection of short stories.

1899   Due to illness, Dunbar and family moved to Harmon, Colorado, where they remained for one year.
Lyrics of the Hearthside, Poems of Cabin and Field.

1900 *The Strength of Gideon, and Other Stories.*
The Love of Landry

1901 *The Fanatics.* Dunbar spent a short time in Florida and
New Jersey before returning to Washington.
Candle-Lightin' Time

1902 *The Sport of the Gods.* Separates from his wife Alice and
returns to Dayton, Ohio.

1903 *Lyrics of Love and Laughter, In Old Plantation Days,*
When Malindy Sings.

1904 *The Heart of Happy Hollow, Li'l' Gal*

1905 *Lyrics of Sunshine and Shadow, Howdy, Honey, Howdy*

1906 Died February 9, in Dayton, Ohio.
Joggin' Erlong

WORKS OF
PAUL LAURENCE DUNBAR

The Best Stories of Paul Laurence Dunbar, B. Brawley, ed. (New
York: Dodd, Mead & Co., 1938).

Candle-Lightin' Time, Hampton Institute Camera Club (New
York: Dodd, Mead & Co., 1901).

Chris'mus Is a' Comin' and Other Poems (New York: Dodd,
Mead & Co., 1907).

The Complete Poems of Paul Laurence Dunbar (New York:
Dodd, Mead & Co., 1913).

and Harry T. Burleigh, "A Corn Song," music by Harry T. Burleigh, lyrics by Paul Laurence Dunbar (New York: Ricordi,
1920).

and Howard Swanson, "A Death Song" (New York: Leeds Music
Corp., 1951).

and Will Marion Cook, "Down de Lover's Lane" (New York:
G. Schirmer, 1900).

The Fanatics (New York: Dodd, Mead & Co., 1901).

Folks from Dixie (New York: Dodd, Mead & Co., 1898).

"Frederick Douglass," *The Monthly Review*, III, 1 (March, 1895).

The Heart of Happy Hollow (New York: Dodd, Mead & Co., 1904).

Howdy, Honey, Howdy (Toronto: The Musson Book Co., Ltd., 1905).

and Will Marion Cook, "In Dahomey" (London: Keith, Prowse and Co., Ltd., 1902).

In Old Plantation Days (New York: Dodd, Mead & Co., 1903).

Introduction to *Thoughts for True Americans* by Richard E. Toomey (Washington: Neale Publishing Co., 1901).

Joggin' Erlong (New York: Dodd, Mead & Co., 1906).

Li'l Gal (New York: Dodd, Mead & Co., 1904).

Little Brown Baby (New York: Dodd, Mead & Co., 1940).

The Love of Landry (New York: Dodd, Mead & Co., 1900).

Lyrics of Love and Laughter (New York: Dodd, Mead & Co., 1903).

Lyrics of Lowly Life (London: Chapman and Hall, Ltd., 1897).

Lyrics of Sunshine and Shadow (New York: Dodd, Mead & Co., 1901–1905).

Lyrics of the Hearthside (New York: Dodd, Mead & Co., 1899).

Majors and Minors (Toledo, Ohio: Hadley and Hadley, 1895).

"Mt. Pisgah's Christmas Possum," *Stories of the South Old and New*, Clarence Addison Hibbard, ed. (Chapel Hill: University of North Carolina Press, 1931).

Oak and Ivy (Dayton, Ohio: United Brethren Publishing House, 1893).

"The Ordeal at Mt. Hope," *Americans All: Stories of American Life*, Benjamin A. Heydrick, ed. (New York, Chicago: Harcourt, Brace and Co., 1941).

and Harry T. Burleigh, "Plantation Melodies, Old and New" (New York: Schirmer, 1901).

A Plantation Portrait (New York: Dodd, Mead & Co., 1905).

poems in *I Hear America Singing,* Ruth A. Barnes, ed. (Chicago, Philadelphia: The John C. Winston Co., 1937).

Poems of Cabin and Field (New York: Dodd, Mead & Co., 1899).

"Representative American Negroes" in *The Negro Problem* (New York: J. Pott and Co., 1903).

Speakin' o' Christmas and Other Christmas and Special Poems (New York: Dodd, Mead & Co., 1914).

The Sport of the Gods (New York: Dodd, Mead & Co., 1902).

The Strength of Gideon and Other Stories (New York: Dodd, Mead & Co., 1900).

The Uncalled (New York: Dodd, Mead & Co., 1898).

"The Unsung Heroes" in *The Poetry of Freedom,* William Rose Benet and Norman Cousins, eds. (New York: Random House, 1945).

When Malindy Sings (New York: Dodd, Mead & Co., 1903).

and Ernest R. Ball, "Who Knows?" (New York: M. Witmark, 1909).

BIBLIOGRAPHY

Aptheker, Herbert, *American Negro Slave Revolts* (New York: Columbia University Press, 1943).

Arnold, Edward F., "Some Personal Reminiscences of Paul Laurence Dunbar," *Journal of Negro History,* XVII (October, 1932).

Botkin, B. A., *Lay My Burden Down* (Chicago: University of Chicago Press, 1945).

Brawley, Benjamin G., *Paul Laurence Dunbar, Poet of His People* (Chapel Hill: University of North Carolina Press, 1936).

Butcher, Margaret Just, *The Negro in American Culture* (New York: Alfred A. Knopf, 1957).

Cady, Edwin Harrison, *The Realist at War; the Mature Years, 1885-1920, of William Dean Howells* (Syracuse: Syracuse University Press, 1958).

Cromwell, John Wesley, *The Negro in American History* (Washington: The American Negro Academy, 1914), pp. 188-194.

Cunningham, Virginia, *Paul Laurence Dunbar and His Song* (New York: Dodd, Mead & Co., 1947).

Du Bois, W. E. Burghardt, *The Souls of Black Folk* (Greenwich, Conn.: Fawcett Publications, Inc., 1961).

Dunbar, Alice Ruth Moore, *The Poet and His Song* (Philadelphia: A.M.E. Publishing House, 1914).

Fauset, Arthur H., *For Freedom, a Biographical Story of the American Negro* (Philadelphia: Franklin Publishing and Supply Co., 1927), pp. 151-161.

Franklin, John Hope, *From Slavery to Freedom* (New York: Alfred A. Knopf, 1947).

Gould, Jean, *That Dunbar Boy* (New York: Dodd, Mead & Co., 1958).

Haynes, Elizabeth Ross, *Unsung Heroes* (New York: Du Bois and Dill, 1921), pp. 41–59.

Henderson, Julia, *A Child's Story of Dunbar* (New York: The Crisis Publishing Co., 1913).

Hughes, Langston, "Paul Laurence Dunbar" in *Famous American Negroes* (New York: Dodd, Mead & Co., 1954).

Johnson, James Weldon, *Along This Way* (New York: The Viking Press, 1933).

———, ed., *The Book of American Negro Poetry* (New York: Harcourt, Brace and World, Inc., 1922).

Lawson, Victor, *Dunbar Critically Examined* (Washington: The Associated Publishers, 1941).

Lotz, Phillip Henry, ed., *Rising Above Color* (New York: Fleming H. Revell Co., 1943), pp. 90–97.

Redding, J. Saunders, *They Came in Chains* (Philadelphia: J. B. Lippincott Co., 1950).

———, *To Make a Poet Black* (Chapel Hill: The University of North Carolina Press, 1939).

Stronks, James B., "Paul Laurence Dunbar and William Dean Howells," *The Ohio Historical Quarterly*, (April, 1958), Vol. 67, No. 2.

Washington, Booker T., *Up From Slavery* (New York: A. L. Burt Co., 1900).

Wiggins, Lida Keck, *The Life and Works of Paul Laurence Dunbar*, (Napervill, Ill., Memphis, Tenn.: J. L. Nichols and Co., 1907).

INDEX

ADDISON GAYLE, Jr., was born in Newport News, Virginia, in 1932. He was educated in the public schools of Newport News and graduated from Phoenix High School in Hampton, Virginia. He received his B.A. from the City College of New York, his M.A. from the University of California at Los Angeles. He is a professor of English at Bernard Baruch College and has written essays, short stories, and reviews for *Teachers College Record, Negro Digest, Phylon, Repartee, The Journal of Human Relations, C.L.A. Journal, Liberator Magazine, Dimensions,* and *Rights and Reviews,* among others. In addition, he is the editor of the anthologies, *Black Expression* and *The Black Aesthetic* and author of *The Black Situation.*